PEACE AND THE CLERGY

PEACE AND THE CLERGY

BY

A GERMAN PRIEST

TRANSLATED BY

CONRAD M. R. BONACINA

"... in praeparatione evangelii pacis"
(Eph. vi. 14)

"... insta opportune importune"
(2 Tim. iv. 2)

NEW YORK
SHEED & WARD
MCMXXXVI

NIHIL OBSTAT : LUCAS WILLEMS, O.S.B., PH.D.
CENSOR DEPUTATUS
IMPRIMATUR : ✠ PETRUS EPUS, SOUTHWARCEN
SOUTHWARCI DIE 17A SEPTEMBRIS 1936

PRINTED IN GREAT BRITAIN

PREFACE

To bring out a book today in support of the Peace Movement might seem a futile proceeding. "Peace Movement"? Does such a thing still exist? And if not (for the moment it seems in fact well nigh wiped out) is it worth while trying to renew the struggle on its behalf?

The author has asked himself this question any number of times. The present work was practically ready for publication more than two years ago. When it was due to appear, however, there took place a violent revulsion of political feeling caused by the revolutionary advent to power of National Socialism in Germany, an event which had immediate repercussions throughout Europe. The post-war period seemed to be liquidated, and a new pre-war period seemed to have begun. The ideas and organizations of the Peace Movement were confronted with a new crisis, and indeed were turned into ridicule by large numbers of people. Once again all experience seemed to speak against them.

But what has this proved? That the peace movement is to be finally regarded as Utopian, and that no one should waste any more time and

strength upon it ?   A *certain type* of peace conception
and peace activity may in very truth be counted as
condemned, though not indeed for the first time, as a
result of contemporary experience.   There have
always been individual enthusiasts who have
believed in the possibility and obligation of banish-
ing any and every use of force from this earth, even
to the point of " submitting to evil " without a fight-
But these few people did not form " the peace
movement " even in the past.   This movement,
whose existence as a force to be reckoned with only
dates back some twenty years, always represented a
very sober and very militant body of opinion both
in the ideas it stood for and in the tasks it set itself.
While never losing sight of its more distant goal for
the future, it busied itself almost exclusively with
the world-political issues of the day, seeking in all
ways possible to redeem these from an all too narrow
partisanship, to have them settled on a higher plane
than that of pure nationalism, to see that justice
was done even to the enemy, to expose the often
sinister backgrounds of groups of interests concerned,
as for example the machinations of armament-
capitalism in the field of international policy
seeking in short to clear the atmosphere, to rid it of
its poisons and preserve it from explosions.   Yet
even this earnest and praiseworthy attempt at the
reform of international life has so far failed to
achieve any substantial result, and some of us are
disposed to think that it will be no more successful

in the future, if it is carried on only by the same means and persons as hitherto.

But what, if this movement were given an entirely different foundation, if it were supported and directed by quite different forces? If Christianity and the Church placed themselves wholly at its service, or rather if the Peace Movement were placed wholly at the service of Christianity and the Church, and on the Church's side similar measures were taken for the spreading and deepening of Peace to those taken for the spreading and deepening of the Faith? We should then be confronted with an entirely new situation. No such Peace Movement has ever yet existed, and it cannot therefore be dismissed with the objections that are urged against the preceding one.

The purpose of this book is to set forth the basic principles of *such* a Peace Movement, to demonstrate its entire agreement with the most elementary ideas and precepts of the Catholic religion, and to call for the enlistment of far stronger Catholic forces in the cause of peace and its world, and against war and *its* world. It is addressed first and foremost to the Clergy as the appointed leaders of every Christian and spiritual mission.

Whether our ideas and demands can be put into execution today or tomorrow, whether this is an opportune or inopportune moment politically to renew the struggle against extreme nationalism and militarism, whether with a fresh move among

Catholics and Catholic priests in favour of world-peace, we shall hear the old reproach of being deficient in patriotism levelled against us once more —these are questions which leave us quite unconcerned. Rather do we follow St. Paul's injunction : " Praedica verbum, insta opportune, importune " (2 Tim. iv. 2), an imperative, which ought never *at any time* to be disregarded, but which today in this particular question certainly appears to be forgotten, if not betrayed. The kingdoms of this world have wrested so much power from the Kingdom of God, they feel themselves so absolutely sovereign, that the followers of Christ have become faint-hearted and no longer dare to stand forth against " Cæsar " with the same resolution as their fore-fathers, indeed have in many cases become infected with his spirit. Here lies the cause of the enemy's strength, and of our own weakness. The enemy is strong, because what he is, he is with his whole heart ; we are weak, because we are neither one thing nor the other. We need more self-assurance, more of the attacking spirit, more readiness to make every sacrifice for Christ.

The author of this book is a German priest. As a work of this kind cannot be published in Germany today, it is appearing first of all solely in an English translation. Its German authorship explains why the majority of the references are to German conditions and to German writers. This however in no wise deprives the book of its universally valid character. For everywhere there is a tension between the Kingdom of God and the kingdom of the world. It can be resolved in favour of the Kingdom of God only through the spirit of those great confessors and martyrs who by their unbending resistance to the powers of this world became heroes and saints. Of such a kind were the two men who were raised to the altar last year :

THOMAS MORE AND JOHN FISHER

To them this modest work is reverently dedicated. May they in our time inspire many Christians with their spirit, especially among those who are called by their vocation to be leaders !

CONTENTS

CONTENTS

CONTENTS

I

THE URGENCY OF OUR MISSION

I

THE URGENCY OF OUR MISSION

It is not necessary to point out that Europe is never safe for two weeks together from the outbreak of another great war. More or less imminent dangers of war rule out the possibility of any real pacification. So long as there are schools, academies, ministries, branches of industry, armies, whose sole purpose is to prepare for war, so long as international politics with all their ramifications never take a step without setting these power-factors in play, so long as natural or artificial tensions exist between States, and "incidents" premeditated or unpremeditated can arise, for the settlement of which there exist no courts with adequate powers of jurisdiction such as operate in the internal affairs of States—so long is the outbreak of another war possible. And because at the present time all these possibilities are to be found at high tension, the danger of war is again today particularly grave.

What a war would be like today, that too is a matter about which the whole world is perfectly clear. The "potentiel de guerre" embraces today practically all existing forces, both material and moral, as there is hardly a single department of the

B 2

national life which remains outside the military sphere, that is to say, which would not be placed at the service of a possible war. And however much the great majority of a people may oppose such an outbreak, they are nevertheless in a dual respect quite powerless to resist it ; they can do nothing against the circle, small in numbers, but supreme in power, of their military, economic and political rulers, and they can do nothing against the gigantic Moloch of the modern machinery of war. The quantitative and qualitative increase in armaments, that is in fighting potentialities, which has taken place during the last fifty years, but especially since the last great war, and which is being daily augmented as no other product of the human mind and will, simply baffles the imagination. It is admitted by all the experts that the mechanical and chemical appliances of war as they exist today can in a short time annihilate not merely whole armies, but whole nations. A tiny minority of people who serve these grotesque instruments of destruction are in a position to overpower and throttle a national majority, be it ever so large and ever so opposed to their views.

That is the *position of the war front.* And the *peace-front ?* First of all, many, perhaps most, of those who stand on the potential war-front will reply that they themselves belong to the peace-front ; that all this merely serves to preserve peace, that it keeps war at a distance by scaring it away. " Si vis pacem,

4

para bellum." To this the Holy Father made answer in his Christmas address in 1934 : " We are ready to believe it. We want *to be able* to believe it and hope it, for the contrary would be too terrible." Everyone feels from these words that the Pope can in fact hardly believe it, and so, in view of the contrary possibility he so greatly fears, he utters the prayer of the Prophet : " Dissipa gentes, quae bella volunt " (Ps. lxvii. 31). But however it be with the will to peace of those who are ready for war, it is quite certain that in hoping to banish war by making preparations for war, they deceive themselves sadly. To begin with, this prescription has never once stood the test of experience in history. Never yet have powerful armies, even when they were of almost equal strength (a parity which is and has always been aimed at) been able to keep themselves mutually in check, i.e., to avoid attacking each other, for any length of time. In 1914, Germany possessed what was acknowledged to be the strongest and best army in the world, but this army—if we subscribe to her own theory that she was attacked or challenged—was not in a position to force the outside world to keep the peace. Secondly, reason, no less than experience, pronounces strongly against the theory that war can be averted by preparing the instruments of war. To enforce peace by the application or threat of force is only possible when the means of power are in the hands of one only of the two contracting parties, not when, as is the case among the States of contemporary Europe, all sides are armed and are more or less on an equal footing. Furthermore, in the feverish establishments built up by the accumulation of the material and spiritual energies of war, there indwells the almost uncontrollable dynamic to fulfil in due course the one specific function for which alone they have been set up. Finally, habitual contact with arms is apt to lead to a spontaneous combustion of explosive material ; through the daily habit of testing and developing the enormous potencies of lethal weapons, there arises a passion for arms which like any other passion presses towards final fulfilment ; and even were this not so—everyone knows that there are many interested parties always ready to produce the explosion *wantonly*.

We see therefore that it is hopeless trying to cast out the devil of war by the Beelzebub of arms— indeed the organized industry for the production and sale of arms is the worse devilry, since a soldier's war is not without an element of nobility free from the purely material and utterly sordid profiteering spirit of the armament industry. It is, as the *Osservatore Romano* remarked in its comments on the Pope's Christmas address mentioned above (26, 27, XII., 1934), a fundamental error to treat the social organism in the same way prophylactically as one treats the human : with inoculation therapeutics ; to use poison to counter poison, to try to drive out war by injections of war. "What is progress in the medical sphere, is a standing-still in the age-old ways, in the political." It is a disgrace that when so much progress has been made in other directions, we should still, after 2,000 years, be adhering in this matter to the methods and expedients of an Epaminondas, a Cicero, a Sallust.

Armed peace as a method of ensuring and consolidating real peace is not worth serious consideration. The attempt to establish and to organize peace on a systematic basis in the same way as war has been systematized, is the aim of *Pacifism*. It is the antithesis of Militarism. Pacifists hold the view that it is not enough to turn away from war with a mere Platonic love of peace, with a frame of mind which is rather an aspiration than a willing and doing, since on the other side there stands not a mere attitude of mind but a widely extended system developed with all the resources of science and technical skill. Ultimately war rests on an instinct, but it derives further support from a right created by this instinct, from a legislation and an endless number of institutions and organizations. Cannot a similar, or rather an opposing, structure be created in the cause of peace ? Does not peace too rest ultimately on an instinct, and cannot the machinery that already exists for the preservation of international peace, and which is comparatively speaking of very recent date, be developed further and more effectively ? Cannot pedagogics, propaganda and organization be placed at its service ? Not, certainly, if the separate States remain as isolated and sovereign as hitherto. But cannot a union of States be formed such as would accord far better with the demands both of nature and of culture ? These are the ideas and aims of Pacifism. It cannot be said that they are rejected *as such* by the majority of men of intelligence and good will. If they nevertheless have no majority behind them, this is due to two main causes. First, it is felt that pacifists are in many ways too radical in their notions and that they often advocate dubious ethical and social theories (strangely enough hardly anyone seems to feel these ethical and social doubts about Militarism !) ; and secondly, the programme itself, even when accepted as right in principle, is held to be impracticable. The latter objection in particular is strongly felt on the Christian side.

On the Christian side emphasis is always laid on the weakness of the human will, the strength of human passions, the imperfection of earthly life, on that great tragedy that attaches to original sin with its ineradicable consequences. This matter will be fully dealt with in the course of this book. All that needs to be said in these preliminary remarks is, that without rejecting the pacifist ideas here set forth, we share the Christian pessimism in regard to all non-Christian endeavours to improve the world. Only, this book sets against this justified Christian pessimism a no less justified Christian optimism, and what is more, a strictly binding Christian *command* which has to be obeyed whatever the difficulties.

However it be with the establishing of " Peace upon earth "—to sit with one's hands folded in face of the difficulties, to let things take their course and do nothing, even when they are heading for a terrible catastrophe, is in no circumstances justified. This kind of passivity is certainly not sanctioned and practised on the Christian side in face of other " ineradicable " evils. But what is of special importance is this : Christians, and not least among them Christian priests, usually answer pacifists in some such terms as these : *You* cannot do it ! Your aims are good, but your means and your people do not suffice ; only Christianity with *its* means and *its* people is capable of bringing peace. The solution therefore must run : " The peace of Christ in the reign of Christ." " This solution "—to quote the words of Otto Schilling, who may be said to express general Catholic opinion on the subject— " implies exactly the same thing that those who uphold the Christian tradition in social ethics have always emphasized, namely that without a return of governments and peoples to the thought of God and to belief in Christ, a realization of the mighty idea of international peace can never be counted on or even hoped for. Hence the Church has always insisted with constant and urgent reiteration that the efforts of the League of Nations in the service of world peace should be based on the thought of

God. Without God's blessing the great work will never succeed. If the Lord builds not the house, if His name is denied, if the representatives of peoples and of States seek to achieve their aims by autocratic methods, if a sincere Christian disposition does not lead hearts back to the spirit and will of righteousness and love, then failure and fiasco without parallel will be the inevitable result." [1] If we have the right to draw the attention of the other side to this decisive truth, we must at the same time admit that we ourselves have hardly placed at the disposal of the peace movement the forces which we alone possess for bringing peace, and the lack of which we affirm on the pacifist side. Schilling himself (well known too as a critic of the Catholic peace movement) writes in the same place : " The whole import and seriousness of this solution and demand (' Pax Christi in regno Christi ') has been, and perhaps to some extent still is, far too little considered and appreciated on the Catholic side."

In fact hitherto it has been practically only small groups of organized Catholic fighters for peace (in Germany the " *Friedensbund* of German Catholics ") who have tried to make the peace command of the New Testament in the modern form which the most recent Popes have given it, the content of a special Catholic action. That they have not made more headway is, over and above their own inade-

[1] Otto Schilling : *Wieder Krieg von Volk zu Volk ?* (Linzer Quartal-schrift 1934, 4).

quacy and the political opposition they have had to contend with, also to be ascribed to the fact that *their flag has not been carried right into the middle of the Catholic camp*, has not been raised as high, say, as the flag of the home and foreign Missions, or as that of the work of social charity. And yet the last two supreme rulers of the Church laid such stress on the peace command of Christ, that the present Pope has, in declared continuance of the peace apostolate of his predecessor, actually made it the leading thought of his Pontificate.

After Pius XI in the Christmas of 1934 had, in view of the constantly increasing danger of a new war, uttered to the world his exhortation to peace, and stigmatized, with unsurpassable severity as " murderous and suicidal madness," the war that was being prepared then, as in the Christmas of 1930, the *Osservatore Romano* (Nr. 299, 1934) took up the Papal appeal with the words : " We must ask ourselves whether for Christianity as faith, idea, action and civilization, the hour of a new decisive birth is not striking in face of the new phenomenon of the suicidal and murderous madness of the nations."

Our book answers this question in the affirmative. It is based on the standpoint that a *new birth of Christianity*, through re-fertilization with the seed of the Gospel, must take place in all spheres, but not least in the sphere of international life. And that if this new birth were to succeed, the Church would be assured of an incomparable increase in honour, gratitude and following. We claim, and shall try to demonstrate with all the emphasis at our command, that in the work for peace and against war, the question at stake is by no means something that merely lies on the periphery of the Church's tasks, but something that is wholly central.

Hence the Clergy must feel that this obligation touches them in a primary degree. The revival of nationalism and militarism after the blows they had suffered in the world war is become so mighty, that it has nearly stifled the strong peace movement that set in after the war, and one might almost despair of trying to combat the new war movement with a new peace movement. But if the danger be so great —and that danger especially which interests us more than the material and physical, the danger to the souls of men and to the mystical body of the Church —then confirmed Christians and consecrated priests, pastors and theologians may not delay to take unto them the armour of God " that you may be able to resist in the evil day, and to stand in all things perfect. Stand therefore, having your loins girt about with truth, and having on the breastplate of justice, and your feet shod with the *preparation of the gospel of peace* " (Eph. vi. 13–15).

The truths which give life to the Catholic struggle against war and the spirit of war on the one hand, and for a union of nations united in justice and love on the other, are sometimes obscured even for priests under a fog of antithetical ideas and by the weight of conflicting facts. Hence our endeavour in the following pages to treat the old truths of our theme in a realistic up-to-date manner, even though it means touching some sore places and grasping a hot iron.

II

THE RELIGIOUS CHARACTER OF THE PEACE MOVEMENT

II

THE RELIGIOUS CHARACTER OF THE PEACE MOVEMENT

(a) THE DIVINE WORLD-ORDER AN ORDER OF PEACE

IF among the movements of the present time there is one which has in many of its parts lost its conscious connection with God, and which yet belongs to Him by its nature, proceeds from Him in germ and presses absolutely towards Him, then it is the Peace Movement. God is a God of peace. There are not many words which express the Divine as truly as " Peace " ; we have only to think of the cosmos which He Himself represents in His Trinity, or of the cosmos of visible and invisible creation, or of the spiritual cosmos of the moral world-order in which rational creatures are meant to lead a harmonious life and find their happiness. In all these orders is Peace, because Peace is nothing but the tranquillity which rests upon every order : " Pax est tranquillitas ordinis " (Augustine) ; not a dead but a living tranquillity, concentrated and fruitful strength, typified in God Himself, and a reflection of His nature, wheresoever it is found. Discord is ungodly, opposed to God's nature and will. Where it shows itself, sin is in play. The first sin broke the original peace, and, as Original Sin, banished it from the earth. But not for evermore. *There is a Redemption!* The Redemption did not remove all the consequences of original sin, nor did it restore the peace of Paradise (though placing it in certain prospect as a new aim for the final consummation) ; nevertheless, through the Grace of the Redeemer, the possession of original justice was again made possible and became for the redeemed a moral obligation. *Thereby peace too became a command.* St. Thomas Aquinas discusses the question whether peace is a virtue, and decides in the negative, on the ground that virtue is not a final end, but a way thereto, whereas peace is an end, a result, a gain, a fruit. At the same time, however, Thomas teaches that peace is a command, for *love* is commanded, of which peace is only an act.

True, what we are chiefly thinking of here is the peace that man enjoys with God and with himself as fruit of the holy love poured out in him. Only, as love of God and love of one's neighbour are one, the children of God must pass on this spiritual peace to the world, must, in human language, help God, so that the external world may again become a Divine order, i.e., possess and preserve peace. Peace already reigns where the Divine order exists undisturbed : in " the starry heavens above us," in the harmony of the spheres, which even for the eye of contemplation creates a profoundly moving impression of sublime peace, and in the (obeyed) " moral law *within* us " (Kant). But God wills too, that peace should reign *around* us : in the *order of society*. For " society is nothing but man extended and multiplied . . . nothing but the projection of conscience into social life." [1] The same moral laws should rule within us and around us. Family, community, State are the organically ascending and self-completing forms of the social order. In this series the State forms in some sort a final term. But it would be a fatal error to regard it as the *last* stage of the God-willed order of society, even in the political sphere. " The human race is despite its division into races and States a unity of a moral *and political* nature," says Francis Suarez,[2] and with him the whole body of Catholic teaching on social theory.

If therefore in the national and internal life of States everything were in order and so in peace, if law and morality ruled in every State, so that all the citizens and associations in each were able to live and develop themselves in a manner worthy of human beings ; but if this harmony within were bound up with disharmony without, if a people and a State loved only themselves and sought their prosperity at the cost of others, if law, justice and

---

[1] K. Werner : *System der christlichen Ethik*, Regensburg, 1850, I., 462.
[2] *De Leg.*, L. II., cap. xix., 9.

love only ruled for them up to their national frontiers, and in their intercourse with their neighbours
they set up in place of strict legality the so-called
right of the stronger, that is the dictatorship of
superior physical force, if, in short, nation threatened
nation with armed preparations, or one claimed for
itself more rights than another—then such a situation,
however satisfactory the internal affairs of each
State might be, would not constitute an order of
society worthy of the name or one that could stand
before God. God wills not only an inner-State
order, but an inter- and supra-State order. It is a
Godless idea and contrary to the Divine Will, to
make the commandment of the equal dispensation
of justice, the commandment of brotherly, co-operat-
ing love and self-sacrificing peace, the commandment
of unity in multiplicity, stop at any political frontiers.
Yet this Godless idea which is so opposed to the
Divine intention holds undisputed sway at the
present time. The international anarchy which at
best places nations and States *side by side* like legal
associations, which reserves to each State the right
to settle its differences with its neighbours not by
way of law but by force, and legalises this procedure
even when the legality has no other basis than the
self-interest of the State concerned and its own
arbitrary political sovereignty—this *legal and moral
vacuum between States* has been for centuries the
condition in which nations live, in juxtaposition to
and confronting each other, not *with* one another :

a caricature of what was present in God's plan from the beginning of the world and has never been displaced therefrom.

(b) THE APPEAL TO ORIGINAL SIN

So strong is the force of habit and so easily does human nature adjust itself to given circumstances, that the great majority of men regard this *bad condition of things as normal*, or, in so far as they feel it to be undesirable, look upon it as unavoidable and unalterable. To this the majority of believing Christians, including their spiritual leaders, form— in practice—no exception. To be sure we have God's vision of the world as a community of nations living together in peace as an ideal picture before our eyes, but to bring it to realisation, this we not only do not regard as our duty, but we look upon it as a sheer impossibility, and that for reasons drawn from our belief in revealed truth.

The original order of society intended by God, so runs the argument, was broken by Original Sin. It is all over for ever therefore with the peaceable community life of different men and groups of men ; doubtless the individual can again find his peace with God and his neighbour, but for the world of nations all such hope is vain. An amazing darkening of the truth of Faith ! Indeed, an amazing effect, too, of the original sin which has brought about this darkening and laming of truth !

The clear truth taught by revelation is this : Original Sin was a terrible catastrophe and in essential parts of its effects an irreparable one. Not only for man as a person, but for human society as well. " Original Sin, in which all mankind through the solidarity of its life and destiny sinned and became guilty, has cancelled for all time, not only for the individual but also for human society, the condition of aboriginal perfection." [1] But what is the conclusion to be drawn therefrom ? According to many it follows that all extra-personal peace, nay, that every struggle for such extra-personal peace, and so for world-peace, is a vain endeavour and a Utopia, which a Christian should properly speaking be ashamed to cherish. In our view it is rather those who think in that way who ought to be ashamed of themselves. Every Christian, and much more every theologian, ought to feel ashamed down to the very bottom of his baptized soul to deduce these consequences from an appeal to the Old and New Testaments. For the Bible teaches something essentially different. It does not teach a radical corruption through the Fall even for *unredeemed* man and corporate humanity (that is the old Lutheran dogma), but only a profound *weakening* of all human forces. " Only through painful toil and struggle could that order henceforward be restored and secured among them, which was bestowed upon

[1] Wilhelm Schwer : *Katholische Gesellschaftslehre* (Paderborn, 1928, p. 50).

their original condition." [1] But in toil and struggle even fallen and as yet unredeemed man could maintain order and peace, indeed he was in duty bound to, and might in no wise deem himself released from the obligation to do so. Even then such a struggle was not regarded as Utopian. Nor was it otherwise in the social order. Community life, too, was profoundly shaken and exceedingly difficult to keep in equilibrium, Cain's fratricide was the first link in a long, heavy chain of raging wars and civil strife ; yet even here every wrong was *avoidable*.

But the decisive fact is, that this unredeemed condition yielded to a wholly new one of *redemption ;* that the curse of the first sin was removed from the earth ; that redemption actually signified a new creation. " The old things are passed away, behold all things are made new " (2 Cor. v. 17). " Again the solidarity of the whole human race enters into operation. . . . Redemption has given to the world a ' holy newness ' (Sancta novitas). In Christ Who brought it, a *new human race* makes its beginning. . . . Yes, what had hitherto been only an *association* of men was raised through Him to a fraternal *community* (Augustine) . . . new forces are poured forth from the Head into man, for the fulfilment of his destiny as a social being also." [2]

[1] Schwer : *Katholische Gesellschaftslehre* (Paderborn, 1928, p. 50).
[2] Schwer : *loc. cit.*, p. 51 ff.

Since, therefore, through the power of redemption, the way to a family of nations united in justice and peace, with Christ the new Adam at the head, again lies open, the appeal to Original Sin as a factor making this impossible is simply inadmissible and contrary to Faith. The weakening consequences of Original Sin have not, it is true, been *quite* removed even from redeemed humanity. But even so, the power of grace is stronger than the power of sin. The grace-filled Christian must still battle with the might of the Evil One ; only faith in grace and grace itself enables him to achieve victory. " This is the victory which overcometh the world, our faith " (1 John v. 4). It is exactly the same in social as in personal life. In his address on " The Structure of Society according to Catholic principles," Georg Baumgartner drew from the " law of sin " and the " law of grace," the following conclusions for social doctrine : " First, there exists no paradise on earth, no world without possibilities of conflict ; second, we confess our faith in *the type of humanity renewed through Christ* and therewith our faith in the *communio sanctorum* and in the Kingdom of God, which, to be sure, we have not to conceive in any sectarian spirit, but rather as an Augustinian *Civitas Dei*, which precisely in our own day stands opposed to a *Civitas terrena* grown to gigantic dimensions." [1]

[1] *Die Ersten Salzburger Hochschulwochen*, 1931, p. 91 (Pustet, Salzburg, 1931).

Here, too, one must believe in the possibility, yes the actuality of the redeeming, unifying, peace-making power of the " gratia capitis." No doubt every " believer " has this belief, in the sense of holding it to be dogmatically true, of giving it his *intellectual* assent. Yet because the mission of the Christianization and pacification of the whole of human society appears so extraordinarily difficult, because after the re-disintegration of the " Christian West," a dividing individualism and nationalism has again raised high its head and now holds political and spiritual sway over the nations, for this reason, that other component of the believer's attitude, the overflowing faith, the confident *surrender* that lays hold not only of the intellect but of the whole man, the optimistic knowledge of the heart concerning the *fulfilment* of the truth held, the Messianic stretching out towards the end which they have surely perceived, does not penetrate to the surface. This accounts for the fact which meets the active worker in the Peace Movement at every turn, particularly from the theological side—that even under the " rule " of grace, people still in a measure groan (literally !) under Original Sin, and continue with perverse obstinacy to base their passivity in the field of social and political reform on the laming effects of Adam's sin, as though, forsooth, Adam were stronger than Christ, sin more victorious than grace, and redemption were reserved for elect souls in a narrowly personal life withdrawn as far as possible from the world, and in an other-world life of glory. What Wilhelm Schwer in his *Katholische Gesellschaftslehre* (p. 229) lays to the charge of a wholly " narrow individualistic conception of the national," that it " contents itself with the comfortless notion that all natural development ends with the nation and that the order of international life is entirely the work of a Divine judgment working itself out in war," this same charge must unfortunately also be levelled against a wholly narrow, individualistic conception of the religious. The ill reception which the revealed commandment of unity and peace has hitherto found among mankind is no doubt to be traced back to the wounding of human nature through Original Sin—that goes without saying ; yet it must no less be attributed also to the fact that this wounding has been exaggerated, not to say cultivated, that its existence has been more strongly felt than the existence of redemption, that the corruption of the earth through the unholy spirit of the world has been more strongly emphasized than its regeneration through the Holy Ghost, indeed, that—strange vicious circle !—the struggle against the consequences of Original Sin, such as for example the Christian peace movement makes its mission in the life of society, has been sabotaged in the name of Original Sin ! One might almost suspect a Mephistophelian trick and joke behind it all. For precisely so can the Prince of this world feel most secure in his dominion.

(c) THE KINGDOM OF PEACE AS END

The power of faith is great, even when the faith is a false one. We see this whenever political aims are set before the eyes of the masses with the driving force of a tremendous faith behind them. They then attract a fabulous following. What lends these movements such a mighty power of appeal, what fills them with such passionate, irresistible, yes, such imposing energy, is their Messianism ! Leaders and led are borne along by what is only comparable to a religious faith in the truth of their doctrine, in the greatness of their mission, in the certainty of redemption in the political kingdom which hovers as an ideal before their eyes and which they love with passionate ardour.

If only because of this faith, this hope and this love, they are bound to prevail over all political opponents who lack these motive forces, no matter though reason, but only cold reason, be on the opposite side. In cultural and political life it is not sober reflection that triumphs, but the strong will drawn by the glittering image of a great end in view, and the fervent heart aflame with a burning desire for this end. The nearness or remoteness of the end plays no decisive rôle in the matter, but only the certainty of its eventual attainment. Indeed a certain remoteness ensures greater directness of aim and concentration of purpose, it prevents wasting time in deliberations, whose proper place is at the journey's end, but which, prior to that, only delay matters and distract attention.

Is the vision of such an ideal objective denied to us Catholic Christians ? Do we only believe in heaven, but not in the earth ? Apart from the fact that Revelation offers grounds for believing that the heaven of the Blessed will have its location on this our earth newly transfigured, our Faith also teaches that for this life too we are to expect an *increasing dominion of Christ in an earthly society formed on an international basis of unity and peace*. The present political system of the world with its internal and external conflicts is not the final form of the life of nations. The leaven of the Gospel will permeate it more and more, improve it and finally perfect it. The line of world-historical development rises and falls, it is true, but even a wavy line with deep hollows may show an upward incline as a whole. That it inclines upward at any rate towards the end, of this we are assured by the prophecies of the Old and New Testaments. Like all prophecies prior to their fulfilment, these, too, lack something in the way of absolute clearness, so that even more than other passages of the Bible they lay themselves open to an erroneous interpretation. As is well known, many *sects* both in the past and now have expounded doctrines regarding the end of the world that are more or less contrary to the Church's teaching. Their error consisted and consists chiefly in the fact that they make the reign of peace of the end-time begin with the *personal* coming of Christ, and that they profess further to be able to give exact accounts both of the beginning and of the duration of this reign. In reality the same revelation which depicts this Messianic reign tells us that the day and hour of its coming is known to no man. Even the " 1,000 years," of which mention is made in the twentieth chapter of the Apocalypse, cannot by hermeneutical rules be taken literally. Yet it is impossible, in the Catholic view, to interpret the whole field of Biblical eschatology, especially that of the New Testament, in a purely figurative sense. Here the clearest pointer lies in what St. Paul says about union in the Faith : Gentiles, Jews and Christians shall form a religious unity (Rom. xi. 25), there shall be " one fold and one shepherd " (John x. 16), even though it may be an incalculably long time before this comes to pass. In his analysis of the various eschatological interpretations, Konrad Algermissen writes : "To-day, of the 1,816 million people who inhabit the earth, only 684 million are Christians, and of these not more than about 330 million are children of the true Church of Christ. Clearly it will be some thousands of years yet before the time comes of which St. Paul speaks, and of which Our Lord says that there will be one fold and one shepherd. It may well be assumed that when at last this glorious time appears, it too will endure for a vast number of years. Only then will the last great prediction be fulfilled." Regarding the millennium the same author says :

"Probably the millennium means a future period of glory and golden age of the Church of Christ here upon earth. The leaven of the Gospel, which is to leaven the whole mass of humanity, has so far been working more or less on the surface. In all probability, we have by far the smallest part of the history of the Church of Christ as yet behind us. According to the words of St. Paul a time will come when the 'fullness of the Gentiles' will have entered the Kingdom of God. Then too all Israel will be saved. The day will have dawned which Our Lord has in view when He speaks of one shepherd and one fold, that reign of Peace which the prophets of the Old Testament depict in such glowing colours. During this reign of peace, the spirit of the saints and martyrs of the old Church will live, as though they sojourned upon earth in their bodies. This golden age of the Church of Christ will be a religious, moral and social regeneration of collective humanity. All evil will be bound. It will be an age prefiguring the glorious resurrection of humanity at the end of time. Hence St. John defines this period as the First Resurrection. This golden age in the history of mankind will last a long time. That is the millennium." [1]

[1] Konrad Algermissen : *Konfessionskunde*, pp. 175–177 ff. (Verlag Joseph Giesel, Hanover, 1930).

Has such a vision of the future no meaning for the present? " Finis est causa causarum," runs a scholastic axiom. That which we desire as our last *end*, determines our whole action, at least if we are persons with a conscious aim. The " last end "— an end without end—of the *individual man*, is the next life, and if he knows what he wills, and wills what he knows, the thought thereof never quite leaves him. But *international life has no next life. Its* final orientation must therefore be the last stage of its development upon earth. If this development is to end in failure, if there is not only no upward movement but only a downward one, then it would wholly accord with the inevitable end, to yield to despair and let things take their course. This helpless passivity may satisfy those who think that international life as we know it today with its hatreds and discords, is in very truth irreclaimable, and rather expect it to get worse instead of better. But for one who believes in the Christian revelation such an attitude is impossible. His faith in the eventual triumph of Christianity, in the certain coming of the " Peace of Christ in the reign of Christ " compels him to lift his eyes towards this high end and to determine his world-political thinking and action by it. It fills him therefore with that Messianic confidence which inspired the pious spirits of the Old Testament, and which, in a secularized and mistaken form, also inspires the people of our own day who strive so passionately

after a political Utopia of the imagination in the
near future. Whoever keeps before his eyes the
"Peace of Christ in the reign of Christ" as his
mission and the certain dispensation of the future,
is never in any doubt as to what is the right policy
to pursue and what is not, which is the straight road,
which goes zigzag and which leads astray. Can
war, for instance, be a straight road to the Messianic
end? It might be, if it created unity, justice and
love. As it produces the contrary, as nothing ever
comes from the use of force, but bitterness, urge for
reprisals and further force, and as, too, its peace-
conclusions are "only another form of force,
conserving instead of attacking," [1] war only throws
back the development towards a better state of
things, and must therefore be banished from
Christian politics as a wrong way and a retrogression.

Let no one demur to our argument on the ground
that the ultimate end of world-history is nevertheless
disaster and ruin, since even the "thousand years"
reign of Christ will be destroyed in the final destruction of the world and in the calamities that precede
it. That is beside the point. Apart from the fact
that this catastrophe is to be conceived as the end-
point, not as the end-phase of historical duration,
and that the death-struggle should no more determine our attitude towards international life than it
does towards human life—the state of maturity

[1] See Leo Baeck : "Judentum und Weltfriede," in the symposium
Religion und Weltfriede (Gustav Engel Verlag, Leipzig).

gives the only right orientation—quite apart from this, the final struggle with resurgent Evil, risen again from out the very reign of Christ, will be waged in a " holy " war for His triumph as Judge of the world, and such a war is in no way comparable with other kinds of wars.

Thus the straight path that leads to peace in and through peace remains the only logical and worthy one for a believing Christian. But who treads this path with calm, unfaltering step ? Not the majority of believers, nor yet the majority of their spiritual leaders. Only they tread it whose hearts have been fired by the religious Peace Movement. Here are the people who see before them the grand world-order of God as an order of Peace. What does it signify that this order is still subject to the severest shocks and that its accomplishment appears so enormously difficult ? A similar difficulty attends the maintaining and perfecting of the order of peace in our interior lives. Yet no conscientious person feels himself absolved from this duty.

It would, we admit, be exceedingly difficult to set energetically to work on a task which it might take hundreds or perhaps thousands of years to master. We have to remember, however, that every work connected with the reform of society proceeds by slow stages, step by step ; it means long, toilsome piece-work, the results of which are not always visible. The endeavour to bring about a more equitable economic order is a case in point. Anyone who cannot live without immediate success should eschew this type of work. Nevertheless, it goes without saying that in working to create the world-order of peace, we are not just working for the distant future. "The peace of Christ in the reign of Christ" will not be effected automatically, through the sudden return of the Lord, as the adventist sects suppose ; but its coming will be, or rather is, an organic development effected through the ever-spreading growth of the tree sprung from "the grain of mustard seed," and through the ever-increasing operation of the "leaven" on the mass of humanity. Accordingly the work we do today towards bringing about this reign of peace is just as necessary, just as effective and just as meritorious as will be the future work of our posterity in the final stage of the development of God's kingdom. Nay more, quite independently of this end, every act of peace has its own intrinsic value as an act of love, and for such acts a person who co-operates in the Peace Movement has a plenitude of opportunities : he can share in spreading the Christian doctrine of peace, in destroying the numerous prejudices and false judgments current in regard to foreign nations, in forming and cultivating friendly contacts between man and man and group and group beyond the national borders ; he can in a word through prayer and labour bring stone upon stone in the building up of God's Kingdom, every one of which would be precious even though this building were continually destroyed and never completed.

No body of men does participation in this labour better befit than the Clergy. Every priest is a " precursor " of the Lord, Who has come indeed, yet still cometh now and at all times, never having finished His way. To make straight His further paths " ad dirigendos pedes nostros in viam pacis," to prepare the way for the full reign of the " Pater futuri saeculi " and " Princeps Pacis " is the vocation and duty of the priest as of none other.

III

CHRIST AND THE PEACE MOVEMENT

III

CHRIST AND THE PEACE MOVEMENT

IF, as we have said, the Peace Movement is a religious movement, and therefore bound up with God, having God as its beginning and its end, issuing from God and leading to Him, then *it must proceed through Christ*. For Christ as the Mediator Who Himself proceeds from God and leads to God, is also the Mediator of everything else that is both of God and is destined for God. It is the culminating revelation in Christ that first makes the Divine absolutely clear. The Old Testament also contains Divine truth, but still latent and undeveloped. Were we, for example, to judge the problem of war and peace by the Old Testament alone, we should certainly apprehend the essential truth regarding it, especially from the prophetic books, but we might easily stick fast in half-truths or even fall into positive errors. Only a rudimentary knowledge of Divine truth was vouchsafed to the people of the Old Covenant; it was the " but I say to you " of Christ that first purified this truth of its dross, and refined it. He laid bare, for example, the problem of marriage and divorce to its very roots, and He exposed the moral identity of hatred

39

and murder. The hater is already a murderer. Everything becomes perfectly clear in its intrinsic value, when measured in Christ. If, too, we measure war and peace in Him, all our doubts scatter at once, darkness and light part in a flash, and peace and the way and the means thereto lie in full daylight. Our judgment is immediate and final.

But it will be well to consider this in detail. The personality of Christ has many sides, and we shall find that no matter to which of these sides we direct our gaze, they one and all of them justify, demand and bless the pledging of our hearts to peace.

(*a*) CHRISTUS REX

Providence has willed that for the Christian consciousness of our time the truth of the Kingship of Christ should once again become a living reality. In the Church itself, this truth had never been forgotten, though even here the figure of Christ the King which dominated the Early Church had receded into the background before other conceptions of Christ. But public and official life, in so far as it was carried on by Christians at all, had in the course of the last few centuries detached itself more and more from the lordship of Christ, and thereby effected a complete return to Paganism. Public life in Pagan antiquity was not without religion, on the contrary it was full of religious associations, but

Pagan religion, in contradistinction to Christianity, was never the master but always only the servant of the State. Christianity had put an end to this idolatry of the State, a fact that found its symbolical expression in the revolutionary refusal of Christian soldiers to offer sacrifice before the statues of Cæsar. " It was the pride and delight of the early Christians that they belonged to Christ, that they were the new people, ' a chosen generation, a kingly priesthood, a holy nation . . . in time past not a people, but now the people of God ' (1 Pet. ii. 9–10). They remained members of the Roman Empire, but they belonged essentially to another. They refused to sacrifice to Cæsar, not for the sake of some idea, but because they had *another* King. For long centuries afterwards this remained the unquestioned assumption of all Christian thinking and doing. It was taken for granted. A Christian was in the first place citizen of the Kingdom of Christ, not member of a nation or even ' citizen of a State.' He gave the family and country his natural love, but his higher essential love was reserved for another world." [1]

The Medieval Empire of the Christian Emperors thus became almost a Christocracy. The idea of the absolute sovereignty of the State was so utterly foreign to it that the Emperor who first dared to propound it, Frederick II, was for this reason

[1] Leonhard Ragaz : *Weltreich, Religion und Gottesherrschaft*, p. 49 (Rotapfel-Verlag, Zürich, München, Leipzig, 1922).

regarded as Antichrist. However, the idea took root and made such progress that it did not restrict itself to *one* claim of absolute sovereignty, but each of the national States that took the place of the universal monarchy made the same absolute claim for itself. Next the process of emancipation extended to the cultural sphere, so that the various " special departments " like science and economics also fell under its sway.

And now the Church has called a halt through Pius XI. At the close of the " Holy Year " 1925, the Pope issued the Encyclical *Quas primas* which developed dogmatically the doctrine of the Kingship of Christ, and cleared up the whole position in relation to the opposing errors. These errors in so far as they concern public life the Pope characterises as " secularism." By this he understands, in a word, the point of view which is prepared at the most to allow religion as a private matter, but which wants to " secularize " public life entirely, i.e., withdraw it from the authoritative influence of religion.

What especially concerns us here is *the position of the State and its politics in relation to the kingly power of Christ*. The Encyclical *Quas primas* does not of course rescind anything of what earlier Church teachers, and notably Leo XIII, laid down regarding the relative *independence* of the State : that the State in its own sphere is absolutely independent of every earthly power including the Church, is indeed in civil and political matters just as " sovereign " as is the Church in her spiritual sphere. But for the State no more than for the Church can there be question of an *absolute* sovereignty, which, perfect in its own right, owes obedience to no higher power. Both State and Church have above them the Divine moral law, which is binding on them in all their measures.[1]

To this the conception of sovereignty of modern political philosophy, which today is the ruling one in practice, stands in clear antithesis : with the result that every Christian is again forced into a position of theoretical and practical opposition. The State can claim respect and obedience only in so far as it subordinates itself to the " eternal and natural law," or at least—if it does not actually affirm this law—does not transgress it through its ordinances. Since God has completed His revelation in Christ, the " eternal law " is the law of Christ. Whether or not *Modern States claim to be religionless, or indifferent to religion or equally representative of all religions—they are and remain bound by the authority of the Son of God.* " It would be a grave error," writes Pius XI, " to say that Christ has no authority whatever in civil affairs, since, by virtue of the absolute empire over all creatures committed to Him by the Father, all things are in His power. Nevertheless,

---

[1] Leo XIII : " Gemina potestas est ; aeternae naturalique legi obedientes ambae," *Nobilissima Gallorum*, February 8th, 1884, Alloc. II., 47.

during His life on earth He refrained from the exercise of such authority, and although He Himself disdained to possess or to care for earthly goods, He did not, nor does He today, interfere with those who possess them. *Non eripit mortalia qui regna dat coelestia* (Hymn for the Epiphany). Thus the empire of our Redeemer embraces all men. To use the words of our immortal predecessor, Pope Leo XIII : ' His empire includes not only Catholic nations, not only baptized persons who, though of right belonging to the Church, have been led astray by error, or have been cut off from her by schism, but also all those who are outside the Christian faith : so that truly the whole of mankind is subject to the power of Jesus Christ ' (Enc. *Annum Sacrum*, May 25th, 1899). Nor is there any difference in this matter between the individual and the family or the State ; for all men, whether collectively or individually, are under the dominion of Christ." [1]

Even Catholics, indeed even Catholic priests perhaps, do not always clearly perceive the consequences of this teaching. It has of course entered into the Catholic consciousness that so-called *Church politics*, under which is understood the regulation of frontier questions between Church and State in internal affairs, must proceed in such a way that no ecclesiastical right, and so in the last resort no command of Christ, is violated thereby (we have grown to be satisfied with this somewhat negative form !) ; but

[1] Enc. *Quas primas*, December 11th, 1925.

that in the *foreign politics* of States no such command must be infringed either, that here too the spirit of Christ must be sovereign—that is a matter which indeed no Catholic would dispute in theory, but which he rarely insists on in practice. We have got used to the fact and tolerate it without demur, that when, for example, an international crisis occurs and diplomatic notes pass to and fro to the accompaniment of the usual journalistic music, the Gospel of Christ is respectfully relegated to the background by Catholic politicians and journalists also. " Reasons of State " have supplanted it or at least hidden it. But what avails it that " Church matters " are fairly satisfactory in the internal affairs of a State, what avails a Crucifix in all schools and public offices, what avails the " Hosanna to the Son of David " in domestic politics, if He is crucified in foreign politics ? But that is what happens particularly in grossly one-sided, purely egocentric handling of conflicts with other countries, in the suppression and falsification of the factors that speak in favour of the foreign standpoint—all naturally " in the interest of one's country." Priests are hardly behind laymen of like " national " sentiments in the allowances they make for such " exigencies of foreign politics." Often too it is far more than making allowances, often it is precisely by priests that oil is poured on the fire of national passions—sacred oil ! For their inflaming zeal actually claims a religious sanction ! " Render to

Cæsar the things that are Cæsar's "—that this sentence is not co-ordinate with its balancing clause, " and to God the things that are God's," but wholly subordinate to it, is in times of national excitement too often lost sight of even by religious people. In such moods an almost unlimited trust is placed in a government which may be far removed from practical Christianity. With what right? In his treatise *Christliches Gewissen und Staatsgewalt* Bishop Emmanuel von Ketteler writes : " The *idea of the sovereign State has its justification ;* but *the idea of the sovereign spirit of man* stands even higher ; for the State passes, whereas the spirit of man is ever-lasting. Both have their origin in God, and so their legitimate correlation, their harmony and order. They should not contradict and deny each other, but respect each other and move harmoniously together in the order which God has assigned to them. If however they were in fact irreconcilable, we *would rather renounce the State than the dignity of man :* better conscientious men without a State than a State with conscienceless men." [1]

We are far too apt to forget that the modern State is fundamentally irreligious or indifferent to religion, and that if it does not thereby altogether forfeit its claim to confidence, respect and obedience, it can at least only lay claim to them in so far as it upholds the rest of the Divine world-order and

[1] Wilhelm Emmanuel von Ketteler's *Schriften*, Band II., *Staats-politische und vaterländische Schriften*, ausgewählt und herausgegeben von Johannes Mumbauer (Kösel a Pustet, 1924).

moral law. I have no confidence in a person who
emancipates himself from God. Nor have I in a
State that does so. I hold myself in duty bound to
regard such a State with profound mistrust and
most of all when it permits itself to encroach upon
the lives of its citizens and upon the rights of foreign
States, as happens in cases of war. We can place
no reliance whatever on the justice of the representations and on the legitimacy of the orders of such
a State ; there is not even the probability that they
will be " just."

Before we obey we must listen ! Listen whether
the voice of God speaks in the command laid upon
us. Sometimes it will be wholly discernible therein,
sometimes not at all, sometimes in part. As regards
the orders that come to us from the supreme
authority of the Church in matters in which she
decides to make use of this supreme authority, we
need not listen in order to obey. There, we know
to start with that God speaks through her. It is
quite different with the State, which declines on
principle to speak in the name of God. Here we
have to listen before we obey, have to test in the
clear light of the commandments of God before we
decide. *Are we not positively forced to doubt, when in a
case of war each of the belligerent governments declares its
cause to be the just one ?* Can the fallibility of political
authority be more strikingly demonstrated ?

All this comes from disregarding the sovereignty
of God in collective official life, especially in the

47

sphere of foreign politics. The indissoluble connection between the recognition of the Divine authority and the political, but also the inevitable collapse of the political when it disregards the Divine, are emphasized in the Encyclical *Quas primas* in the following words : " If the rulers of nations wish to preserve their authority, to promote and increase the prosperity of their people, they will not neglect the public duty of reverence and obedience to the rule of Christ. What we said at the beginning of Our Pontificate concerning the decline of public authority, and the lack of respect for the same, is equally true at the present day. ' With God and Jesus Christ,' We said, ' excluded from political life, with authority derived not from God but from man, the very basis of that authority has been taken away, because the chief reason of the distinction between ruler and subject has been eliminated. The result is that human society is tottering to its fall, because it has no longer a secure foundation ' " (Enc. *Ubi arcano*).

Who then is to put us on the right way again ? The Church, you will answer. Yes, but this answer is too general. At the present time, in contradistinction to the Middle Ages, the Church concentrates her energies on the " spiritual," marking it off with sharp emphasis from the " temporal." That in interior force and spiritual momentum she has greatly gained thereby, is not to be doubted. The historical situation also urges this attitude upon her. If in former times, it was possible to reproach the ecclesiastical hierarchy up to the highest ranks with striving for temporal power to the injury of the spiritual, it is all to the good that the Church today, when such complaints have become entirely groundless, should avoid even the appearance of wishing for a return of those times. Of course "*temporal rule*" *must not be confused with the rule of Christ over all temporal things*. To bring about this rule of Christ must always be the Church's constant endeavour. But the secularized world of today is not ripe for such a conquest. In the meantime freer, looser forces than the official-ecclesiastic must prepare the way. And here an important mission lies before a Catholic *policy*. Its orientation is essentially "temporal," pertaining to civil life, but at the same time spiritual, Christian, Catholic, and it can and should build a line of communication between the Kingdom of God and the kingdom of the world. There is no lack of such a Catholic policy, even though, as has been said, it unfortunately restricts itself almost entirely to internal affairs, instead of handling foreign-political problems with the same energy in the Catholic, i.e. supra-national spirit (all rootedness in the national life notwithstanding). Nevertheless politics can never function unhampered. Even " a Catholic policy in the widest sense stands as means far below the Catholic idea." [1] This is

---

[1] Friedr. Schreyvogl, *Katholische Revolution*, p. 7 (Der neue Geist-Verlag, Leipzig, 1924).

owing to the constraining force of compromise and limitation to which all politics is subject. In the metaphysical reality of ideas one can move with perfect freedom, but in the area of politics one strikes against the physical reality of things. In addition there is the limitation imposed by the area of the State and of the Party. Politics has to do with a definite government, a definite parliament, definite laws, and since too, it can hardly work otherwise than in or with a party, it is further handicapped by the machinery of such party. Not infrequently the party political machine operates so centripetally that it refuses to adopt the good ideas of another party, as party prestige forbids it.

What remains over then, if neither the official Catholic Church nor the Catholic Party can strike out with absolute freedom beyond the reality of existing conditions? *The Catholic "Movement."* It is not bound by "hard facts," but is called to transcend them, to build the facts of the *future*. Whereas politics must sow today and reap tomorrow, the "Movement" works with a long view. The "Kingship of Christ" in the form in which the Papal Encyclical describes and demands it, is so far removed from contemporary reality, that politicians cannot include it in their plans at all, and even the ecclesiastical authorities, apart from the Papacy, cannot work for it *directly* (though indirectly of course). But that is precisely what the Catholic Movement and especially the Catholic

Peace Movement can do. In so far as it is a "peace movement," it has to fight day in and day out for peace and against war ; in so far as it is a "Catholic" peace movement, it has to carry on this struggle entirely in the spirit of Christ and of the Church. It is thus the particular mission of such a movement to influence, with the help of the clergy, religious life in a specific direction. The majority even of religious Catholics are only religious in the sense of a personal spiritual culture. For them religion consists in the satisfactory relationship of the soul with God and His world beyond. It is that conception or at least application of religion that has provoked Leonhard Ragaz to take as his watchword : "Not religion, but Kingdom of God ! " By religion he understands the sum of doctrines, usages, practices, which form a "world for themselves alone " cut off from the rest of the world. By "Kingdom of God " on the other hand, he understands what Moses, the prophets, and Jesus also, strove for: not a purely-spiritual, purely-religious thing hovering as it were between heaven and earth or something isolated in the world, but a new "world-condition born of God " embracing in itself the entire world, "as tangible and visible as the Roman Empire, though the exact opposite thereof in its fundamental nature and, as goes without saying, with all its realism, of an infinite spirituality." [1]

---

[1] *Loc. cit.*, I., 142 ff. Because "religion " in contradistinction thereto has a tendency to "become something which is right for its

Pius XI has insisted on the Kingdom of God *around* us in a manner perhaps that has had no parallel since the Middle Ages. He has called upon all the faithful to set up the " Kingdom of Christ " again in the modern world notwithstanding all the obstacles in the way of it. While making this appeal, however, he also complains of " a certain timidity and slowness in good people, who are reluctant to engage in conflict or oppose but a weak resistance." It may be said perhaps that the bulk of these " good people " make no response to such an appeal not from any lack of good will, but because they are not cut out for pioneer work and combative activity. To this there is a twofold reply. In the first place proper means must be taken to bring the call to their notice. Is the Pope's demand for soldiers for the Kingship of Christ being brought home to the laity in an adequate manner ? Latterly this is being done here and there through " *Catholic action*." But this action too usually remains a very perfunctory and superficial activity. Yet today, especially in the world of young men, the demand for the Christianization of public life meets with a quite exceptional response, and the idea of peace

own sake," and to leave this world to take care of itself, Ragaz inveighs passionately against such pietistic " religion." The Protestant has more grounds for doing this than the Catholic, since the Catholic religion knows no such abstraction of the " worldly," but is at pains to subjugate this world to itself as Kingdom of God. It has to be admitted, however, that in *practice* this universal tendency is not very marked even with us. The Kingdom *above* us and *within* us is what most of us are most deeply concerned with rather than the Kingdom around us.

in particular, when expounded in all its grandeur and chivalry, finds a positively enthusiastic following.

The " pious " life, as every priest knows, does not make a particularly strong appeal, largely because it is conceived almost entirely as a life of inwardness and withdrawal. The " worthy," the meek, the prudent, the considerate and retiring—these are the types of a predominantly inward piety. And they meet with little sympathy among strenuous people of a vigorous forceful temper. It is only the taking part in great movements which discover new worlds to conquer, that awakens the interest of active men and women and makes Christianity a modern and sympathetic religion for them. What energies the struggle against a State which does not respect the higher rights of God's Kingdom can unloose, was seen, for example, at the time of the *Kulturkampf* in Germany. That was, as we know, only possible because the clergy refused to make any concessions to the State in the sphere of ecclesiastical prerogative, but stood manfully by the rights of Christ. The same thing would happen if the clergy set themselves against a nationalism and militarism sanctioned by the State but menacing to world-peace.

If, however, the majority of well-intentioned Catholics could not really be won over by the clergy for a pioneer-work that means swimming against the stream, then at any rate the clergy *themselves* must undertake it. It is incumbent on them in the first degree not to rest content with things as they are, but to push forward the Kingdom of God. Friedrich Schreyvogl calls this the "Catholic Revolution." "Every revolution is preceded by an avowed faith in some supra-real plan which exists independently of every given fact and breaks free from the force of its consequences. When it ripens to action it puts what is *willed* in place of what *is*, the influence of a higher will in place of what would follow naturally in the logic of events. Every true revolution expresses a lofty revolt of the person against the thing, of the man against the work, of faith against experience.[1] The will to the building up of a better future world is the truest preparation for a struggle against the prevailing current." [2]

A yearly stimulus to the renewal of such a spirit and will is provided by the new Feast of Christ the King. Here blows the Messianic air of the future as in perhaps no other office of the ecclesiastical year. Messianic peace, Messianic lordship over all nations, pride, joy and confidence are the content of this glorious Feast. It should be made the patronal Feast of the Catholic Peace Movement ! In many places it is preceded by a triduum, a good opportunity for setting forth and appraising the wealth of ideas contained in the Kingship of Christ. This the priest should use to invest his priesthood with a

---

[1] But we may also say : Of the thing against the person, of the work against the man, of the ideal namely against the reality.

[2] *Loc. cit.*, p. 9.

prophetic character, and to help realize with his flock the promise : " Multiplicabitur ejus imperium, et pacis non erit finis " (Ant. ad Nonam).

(b) CHRISTUS PASTOR

In the world of Messianic ideas Christus Pastor means almost the same thing as Christus Rex. The " kings " of the Old Covenant were " shepherds," because their riches consisted of wide pasture-lands and herds, and because too they fed the people like docile sheep. Thus if Christ calls Himself the Good Shepherd, it is because the chosen people—at first a community of race, but later one of faith—belongs to Him, and because He gives His life for the community with the absolute devotion of a good shepherd.

This sublime conception of sovereignty and possession adds something to kingship which is not inherent in the idea itself. Indeed sovereignty as a rule stands in direct contrast to service and selfless love. Christ, however, proclaims a new type of kingly dignity and kingly duty. " You know that the princes of the gentiles lord it over them : and they that are the greater, exercise power upon them. It shall not be so among you, but whosoever will be the greater among you, let him be your minister. And he that will be first among you, shall be your servant." Jesus was the first king in the world who acted according to this principle : " Even the Son of Man is not come to be ministered unto, but to minister " (Matt. xx. 25–28).

Thus Jesus, the " King of the eternities," became the loving ministering Good Shepherd of all men. He became their friend, benefactor and saviour. What concerns us here is the way He manifested this love where it is found least among men : in personal and national oppositions, in the domain of the passions which separate men and nations from each other and drive them to mutual destruction.

In the first place, it is to be noted that Jesus did not exclude from His pastoral love *soldiers*, who stand forth as the exponents of political and national oppositions. There was no native soldiery in the Palestine of those days, but only a foreign one, inimical to Jewish national feeling : the Roman garrison troops. We know with what eyes a foreign army is regarded by the population whose territory it occupies. The complete social ostracism of the foreign soldiers is felt to be demanded by the national honour ; friendly intercourse with them would be destructive of national dignity. It should not be condoned even when a Christian layman allows his head and heart to be turned by national passion, but in a priest it deserves the severest condemnation. *Sacerdos alter Christus !* The personal and professional honour of the priest and the vocational duty of the spiritual pastor as an image of the Good Shepherd imperatively demand that patriotism and the national honour, under cover of which the gravest

crimes are committed, be wrested from their pagan
savagery and baptized with the spirit of Christ.
The priest can and should love his country, but only
as a part of the Divine world-order, as a community with praiseworthy merits and blameworthy
faults, called and in obligation bound, in virtue of
the commandments of God, to be a shield of order,
right and welfare in the framework of the comity of
nations. This obligation further implies the proper
appreciation of other countries and their inhabitants,
whether the latter remain in their own land or come
as foreigners into ours. As regards soldiers Christ
teaches us first and foremost not to despise their
profession. Were this profession irreconcilable with
the spirit of His Gospel, He would have said or
hinted as much in His meetings with soldiers. *A
Christian and a Christian peace movement, cannot participate therefore in any discrimination against the military
profession as such,* but only in the task of reducing it
to the limits of *true order and justice*.

Soldiers, even those of an " enemy " nation, are
human beings ; their souls should mean as much
to the spiritual pastor as those of other men ; nay,
inasmuch as in a foreign country they are the target
of hostile feelings, the pastor of souls ought to make
them his special care and let them feel that with
the priest the hostile foreign country leaves off and
the friendly Kingdom of God begins. This was the
experience of " enemy aliens " in the native land
of Jesus. As noblest son of His people the foreign

rule of the Romans could not be indifferent to Him, but He did not speak of it. His wonderful soul was free of all bitterness on that point, however deeply it might feel the humiliation of His fatherland. But Jesus knew : it was deserved ! His Father in heaven knew what He permitted to happen ! His Providence was eternally holy ! And the Roman soldier—how could he help it ? So the officers and officials of the foreign occupation might come to Him, and His heart stood as open to them as to any of His own countrymen. Whether any Jewish nationalist with his narrow sullen contempt for every non-Jewish creature ever converted a Roman to the religion of the true God, we do not know. It is not very probable. But the two Roman officers whom Jesus of Nazareth met, were converted. True it was His Divinity that changed their hearts, nevertheless it was done through the medium of His great humanity. When a person lacks this humanity, his patriotism can only repel, never attract. Such an one is the worst possible awakener of foreign sympathies for his own country. He, on the other hand, who meets the foreigner and even the foreign soldier with loving-kindness, serves as does no other patriot the true interests of his native land.

To cherish kindly feelings towards all men should not however cause us to cherish without further consideration the same kindly feelings towards the thing they serve and perhaps must serve against their will. Soldiers are not the same thing as a military régime. Towards the latter the disciple and still more the Vicar of Christ must preserve a very critical attitude indeed. The military system gains friends among us because it presents itself as a system of order, and of protection and " defence " against bad neighbours. This is not the place to expose all the devilry that can conceal itself behind the " defence spirit," the whole materialism of militarism, its militaristic outlook and its material equipment grown to such monstrous proportions in the hands of armament-capitalism. All that calls for remark here is that a leader of the people like the spiritual pastor and the moral theologian must see through the falseness and deception of militaristic ideology and phrase-making. He remains first and last and all the time priest and steward of Jesus Christ. For him, too, holds good Christ's saying that no man can serve two masters. Christ wills indeed that we also serve " Cæsar," but in a new regenerate spirit vitally corrective of the old. This means that the *unlimited* authority of " Cæsar " is now finished and done with. Henceforward its absoluteness breaks upon the Christian conscience ; where it falls foul of that, it has to yield.

Thus the spirit of Christ must also enter into legitimate rights of sovereignty like that of self-assertion. As the natural order has not been abrogated by the supernatural order which Redemption has re-established in the world, it follows that

the question of *defence* or *resistance* has also remained
in its natural right. The Gospel does not forbid
even armed resistance against unlawful aggression.
At the same time we cannot ignore a remark of Our
Lord's which He addressed not to an aggressor, but
to the defender of a just cause : " Put up again thy
sword into its place : for all that take the sword
shall perish with the sword " (Matt. xxvi. 52).
This saying must not be pressed too far, and we
cannot deduce therefrom an absolute prohibition to
take the sword. Nevertheless it contains the deep
truth and prophecy which has been fulfilled thousands of times in the course of human history : that
the use of force invariably calls forth the use of
further force and consequently has something self-
destructive in its very self. Certain it is that Christ
wished to redeem and baptize, i.e., christianize the
notion of resistance. The Christian religion cannot
take over without further ado the usual methods of
settling personal and international differences, it
must seek to overcome bloody by unbloody methods
and *to create confidence in spiritual and religious methods
of defence*. Even the Old Testament revelation is
full of warnings against putting one's trust in steeds
and chariots, towers and physical strength ; it is
spiritual and religious, not material forces that
guarantee victory and salvation. True enough, this
trust in God did not exclude the application of
warlike measures, but apart from the uniqueness and
incomparableness of the theocratic circumstances,

with which no later war can be compared, it is precisely the history of Israel's wars that should expose a truth of most vital importance, the inadequacy of all material might as compared with the arm of God, which helps so much the more, the less one relies on other aids. Moreover, the Gospel knows nothing of warlike power even as *means* to the end (of the Kingdom of God). In fact, at its culminating point, the Sermon on the Mount, the ideal it sets up is the absolute antithesis of the military way of thinking. " The Gospel, focussed wholly on the inwardness of the love of God and one's neighbours, which includes love of one's enemy as a matter of course, utters in its Magna Charta, the Sermon on the Mount, a terrible warning against the mighty, powerful and violent ones of this earth and extols as blessed an attitude which is diametrically opposed to every warlike disposition." [1]

Against such ideas and demands the objection is often raised that they are impossible to carry out in this world of sin. It is strange that this reason, particularly on the part of priests, is not likewise brought into play against other ideals and commandments of Christianity, against, for instance, the commandment of chastity, which is so extremely difficult to carry out and is daily transgressed by millions. Here nothing but the strictest observance of the command is ever tolerated. How far this analogy is justified we shall see later. The point

[1] I. P. Steffes, *Die Abrüstung*, p. 21 (Gilde-Verlag, Köln, 1932).

to be noted is this : the spiritual director, as Christ's servant and representative, is in duty bound to possess and preach the spirit of Christ, no matter how it may stand with the obligation and distinction of difficult and easy duties in individual cases. In no circumstances may the priest pass over ideals such as the spiritualization and christianization of the conception of defence, with the frivolity, the ridicule and cynicism, that the " world " is pleased to treat them with. When, for example, the demand for *disarmament* is raised, one can, as a person who knows the world and as a Christian of deep-rooted faith, harbour the gravest doubts as to the seriousness and the success of this demand, *in so far as it is sponsored by political and military leadership*, but the idea itself one must make one's own, and hold fast to it, even though it fail of realization a thousand times. It fails only because ill will has been at work, not because it could not be carried through with good will. We must condemn the lack of good will, not the idea. A disciple of Jesus Christ always knows how great is the disparity between his ideals and the reality. But he does not surrender these ideals and their obligations on that account, but upholds them with firm confidence. He knows no compromise with false ideas. He knows compromise with facts ; with the fact that many persons strive against the good out of weakness or malice—he understands such persons, treats them with gentleness and patience, hopes for their improvement ; he knows that often one can only attain the good, step by step, he knows therefore *halting-places* and *intermediate ends* on the way to the final end, but he never loses sight of this last. The religious man is also free from the short-sightedness and short-livedness of those who see only yesterday, today and tomorrow. What happens or does not happen in these short stretches does not even prove anything for or against the whole of reality, let alone anything for or against supra-temporal truth. Even if this truth is not regarded and followed at the present time, and never has been in all past history, it may yet be realized in the future, and though it never be realized, truth still remains truth.

It would be far from right, however, to make the wicked " world " alone responsible for the scant attention that is paid to the spirit of Christ. In considering the question of the so-called " impracticability " of certain evangelical ideas, we have further to ask ourselves whether Christians and their spiritual directors *are not themselves to blame for the situation that has arisen*. Which of us has up to now striven to bring about a more Christian formation of international relationships ? Which of us has earnestly put the weight of his priestly authority on the side of those who have endeavoured to replace the system of " armed peace," i.e., of perpetual military intimidation, by a better one. Is not the alleged " impracticability " of a situation of international justice and peace to be traced back in part at least to the fact that the efforts to achieve this end *have lacked the moral support of those who have in great measure had in their hands the forming of public opinion and the guidance of the well-meaning population ?* We personally are thoroughly convinced that this is not only *one* reason, but the chief reason for the " impracticability " of better international relations : I mean the failure of so-called " good people " more than the failure of so-called " bad people." It is the shepherds who have been found wanting, not so much the flock. For the flock loves peace if only for the sake of its own prosperity. All conflicts menacing to peace come from the leaders, they are worked up and made to explode by them. As a rule the minister of religion has nothing *directly* to do with them ; his share of the guilt begins when he tries to explain these proceedings in almost fatalistic fashion—as somehow the unavoidable " consequences of original sin "—when he lets them take their course and dismisses the peace movement with a smile of ignorance and a shrug of the shoulders as Utopian. This is still the normal attitude among the clergy, in spite of the totally different spirit that has inspired the utterances of recent Popes. It will be shown later how damaging this is to the prestige and influence of the clergy, how large numbers of the faithful flock have had their trust in their pastors shaken thereby and are beginning to turn away from them.

If militarism and the mental dispositions akin to

it continue to load the atmosphere with tension, then sooner or later *war* must break out. The times in which we live can still be described as " post-war," since we are still suffering from the baleful consequences of the Great War. What Benedict XV wrote in his Encyclical *Pacem Dei* in the year 1920 holds good even today : " To the mind of anyone who sees this picture of misery by which the human race is oppressed there must come back at once the story of the Gospel traveller who was journeying from Jerusalem to Jericho and fell among thieves who robbed him and covered him with wounds and left him half-dead by the wayside. The two cases are very much alike ; as to the traveller there came the good Samaritan, full of compassion, who bandaged his wounds, pouring oil and wine over them, took him to the inn and undertook all care of him, so to cure the wounds of the human race the hand of Christ Jesus is needed, of Whom the Samaritan was figure and image." And now comes the *appeal to the bishops :* " Therefore we pray you, Venerable Brethren, and we exhort you in the bowels of charity of Jesus Christ, do everything in your power, not only to urge the faithful entrusted to you to lay aside hatred and pardon offences, but also to promote more actively all those works of Christian benevolence which bring aid to the needy, comfort to the afflicted, protection to the weak, opportune assistance, in fact, of every kind to all who have suffered most gravely through the war.

We wish that you should specially exhort your *priests, as ministers of peace, to be assiduous in this work,* which is indeed the very compendium of the Christian life, *in preaching love towards one's neighbours, even if enemies,* and being ' all things to all men.' *So as to afford a shining example, let them wage war everywhere on enmity and hatred,* knowing well that in doing so they are doing a thing very welcome to the most loving Heart of Jesus and to him who, however unworthy, is His Vicar here on earth."

These words of the Pope might serve as motto for our book. They contain an urgent entreaty to the whole clergy to work everywhere with untiring zeal against war and the war-spirit, and for peace. It is works of corporal and spiritual mercy that are here called for. Critics of the Peace Movement sometimes reproach it with a certain softness. With heroic reference to the significance of suffering in the Divine world-plan and for the way of salvation, they dissociate themselves as Christians from a " humanitarian pacifism." Ought one to take them seriously ? There does exist a " humanitarian " outlook that is to be repudiated. For the use of language has so narrowed the word " humanitarian," which in itself means nothing but " philanthropic," that it has come to denote a purely natural love of men without supernatural reference, without, therefore, the love of God. Accordingly by " humanitarian " is usually understood the sort of disposition which ministers to purely worldly welfare. Such a tendency might pass, were it not that it sometimes appears in express *opposition* to Christian charity and actually claims to replace Christianity by an enlightened and therefore higher " noble humanity." It is doubtless in *freemasonry* that this tendency has its spiritual home.

Of this humanitarian love of men Max Scheler says sharply : " It is primarily the form of expression of a suppressed denial of, and impulse against, God " ; he even goes so far as to call it the " cloak for a suppressed hatred of God " ! It may be that not a few modern people in the Liberal and Socialist camps draw their pacifism also from such sources : a love of peace solely from love of humanity to the exclusion of the love of God. We Christians are convinced that a real and genuine love embracing the whole person, can only exist where the Creator, Preserver, Redeemer and Judge of this person, God, is included in our thinking and willing, and we therefore regard purely humanitarian strivings as inadequate, yes as reprehensible. But to restrict human love at the cost of Divine love, or to think that, because God has permitted sufferings of every kind, we are thereby prohibited from fighting against these sufferings with the same energy and determination as the " humanitarians," would be a no less reprehensible error. The spectacle wherein the orthodox priest and Levite beholds humanity stricken and flayed by war and passes callously by, leaving it to the heterodox Samaritan to take charge of it with compassionate love, must not be allowed to occur. Nor of course has it occurred in this crass manner. After war had inflicted its terrible wounds on mankind, Christians and Christian priests tended them just as devotedly as did the representatives of so-called pure humanity. Only we still have to ask ourselves the humble question whether we have been at equal pains not merely to *heal* war-wounds, but to *prevent* them, and whether at any rate this is so today. We are thinking of the systematic struggle against war and its range of ideas.

Here antipathy to "humanitarianism" has a considerable say in our counsels.[1] So, too, has the strange notion that a very decided opposition to war is hard to reconcile with a patriotic outlook, which in turn is not seldom identified with a militarist outlook. The priest in fine might get the idea that he is merely a pastor of souls, not of bodies, and that consequently the physical misery of war does not directly concern him. Whoever thinks that, had better let himself be taught differently by Christ,

[1] In his book, *Friede auf Erden?* Superintendent-general (of the clergy) Otto Dibelius has a special chapter on the "Peace of inferior (*gemeinen*) natures." With many of his pronouncements we agree. On the other hand, much of what he stigmatizes as efflux of an "inferior nature" is nothing but a justifiable and necessary revolt against the miseries of war senselessly and irresponsibly brought on or "endured." When Dibelius refers contemptuously to the strong desire for peace that made itself increasingly felt among the stricken people at the close of the world-war, as the "peace-ideal of inferior natures," as the demand of those who "know only eudaemonistic ends in life," he can hardly be surprised if he meets with a furious reply in a Socialist newspaper (*Das andere Deutschland*) and if his disdainful judgment brings grist to the mill of those who dismiss the Church as the ally of militarism and as the enemy of the people.

the Good Shepherd. His cure of souls began as a rule with a benefit for the body. The human being entrusted to our care cannot be split into soul and body, indeed the way to the soul through the body is in most cases not a roundabout way, but the quickest and surest. What Emanuel von Ketteler laid down at the Episcopal Conference at Fulda as the basis of all effective pastoral work among the working-classes, holds good for pastoral work among suffering humanity generally : " As long as such a working-class is only offered the graces of Christianity along the usual lines of pastoral ministration, it will remain as a whole completely insensible and inaccessible to them. *Steps must first of all be taken to humanize these brutalized people before we can think of christianizing them.*" By no one, not by the Quakers and still less by unbelieving Socialists, ought we priests to allow ourselves to be surpassed in the fierce struggle against inhuman social conditions ; and the same with the fight against the homicidal monster of war which adds so immeasurably to the sufferings of this world ; rather ought we to take our place in the front rank of the opponents of war. The reproach of not being whole-hearted in the national cause will only impress a priest of weak character. It shows in him a lack of Christian and priestly dignity, which towers as high above the national dignity as heaven towers above the earth, to make the ideal of the " nation " the measure of his moral conduct. Where the word "national" has acquired the meaning which only the word "religious" possesses for us— the expression of final orientation, of deepest feeling and willing—we should declare our entire agreement with those who deny us *this* sort of national sentiment. The banner of unchecked nationalism is stained through and through with blood, often with the blood of brothers shed criminally, crying aloud to heaven, and with countless other stains as well. Moral and Christian cleanness bids us keep some distance away from this standard. For the rest the priest serves the community in excellent measure by the fact alone that he is a good priest. Any special "national" profession and activity is superfluous, and in view of the peculiar flavour the word national has acquired, distressingly awkward.[1]

War offers great opportunity for moral achievement, yes for real heroism. This no one will gainsay. The over-emphasis of this truth must be balanced, however, by exposing the bad reverse side with equal clarity, the more especially as the dark side of war far overshadows the bright. The physical and spiritual miseries of war and its aftermath work on each other. It would require a separate book to paint the whole picture. Here it must suffice to throw a passing light on the *moral* misery, which must concern us priests even more than the bodily. During the years 1915–1919, the number

[1] For the positive aspects of national qualities and peculiarities see the chapter on "Patriotism" in *The Church and War* (Sheed and Ward, London.)

of young persons sentenced for criminal offences in Prussia alone rose from 70,000 to 150,000. Thus we see that even back in the interior of the country the war increased moral lawlessness by more than double. How was it at the front? During the war of 1870–71, 32,500 soldiers had to be treated in hospital for venereal disease. In the world-war, the number was 800,000! We can well imagine what the total number of persons guilty of adultery and fornication must have been, if that figure merely represents those who contracted venereal disease. These sins do not take place only in war, but in war, in the presence of death, they manifest a peculiar ethical barbarism. From this, the priest must see for himself that he can hardly escape the reproach of ignorance and empty phrase-making, when in his sermons he himself describes every soldier in a general way as a " hero." When shall we put an end once and for all to the twofold standard of measurement whereby one rule is applied to anything connected with the nation and war, and another to what takes place outside these categories?

It is with reluctance that we dwell further on the appalling multiplication of sins that ensues from war and its attendant system. There is not a *single* commandment which is not trampled under foot an incalculable number of times more often through war than without it. We will confine ourselves to one. The offences against the sixth and ninth commandments, of which mention has just been made, are those to which spiritual directors usually pay most attention. We need not waste words in pointing out that here, in fact, lies a main source of danger for faith and morals ; it is a matter therefore with which we cannot concern ourselves too much, and which demands our most serious attention not only on its moral-theological, but also on its biological, psychological and sociological sides. But it is not the most important matter. A right understanding of moral and pastoral theology demands that we take *the fifth commandment even more seriously than the sixth*. For both logically and ethically the fifth ranks above the sixth. Its object stands higher : life and love. Grave as is the command : " Thou shalt not commit adultery," graver still is the command : " Thou shalt not kill," and its positive counterpart : " Thou shalt love " ! Thou shalt above all fulfil the " first and greatest commandment " : which is to love God and love thy neighbour. But our " neighbours " also include our political enemies.

As regards the fulfilment of this commandment, it is certainly no less difficult than that of the sixth. Is there any justification for insisting more strongly on the keeping of the sixth ? No. Is this done, however ? Yes, everywhere ! It will be said, perhaps, that the *consequences* of impurity are worse than those of lawlessness. But how ? With slight transgressions of either commandment, the consequences are slight, with grave ones grave. We are here concerned with the case of war. How far war itself is a grievous sin against the fifth commandment, and how far it is not, is a question we cannot go into here.[1] It is sufficient to remind ourselves that Catholic morality recognizes certain conditions for the permissibility of a war, which the warmongers themselves do not bother about in the least. If a single one of these conditions is not fulfilled, the war is an unjust war and a sin crying to heaven for vengeance. Will anyone deny further, that even in the framework of a " just " war, the fifth commandment may be transgressed in a thousand ways, and is so transgressed ? And that even without war, the air produced by it and producing it is full of the seeds of hatred, of the most violent anger, revenge, vilification, all sins which Christ condemns with the utmost severity and threatens with hell fire ? In what way are these passions that violate the fifth commandment less evil and dangerous than those against the sixth ? Whence do we priests derive the right to combat the disordered irascible passions less strenuously than the concupiscible ones ? Every sin against love is a " peccatum mortale ex genere suo."

And must it always be a mortal sin that calls our pastoral care into action ? Nationalist passion is not necessarily grievously sinful. It would be going too far therefore to suggest that it alienates as

---

[1] Cf. *The Church and War*, Section III. " War as a Metaphysical and Moral Problem," pp. 69–116.

many souls from Christ as does the sexual. It is none the less true, however, that the nationalist fever threatens to separate *more deeply* from Christ those whom it seizes than does the sexual. Sexual sin proceeds from human weakness ; the higher reaches of the soul need hardly participate therein, indeed the spirit may be willing to resist, while the flesh is weak. The commandment of purity itself is not denied by the sinner of this type, it is not treated with contempt, but is perhaps reverently acknowledged. From such a person, who feels himself a " poor sinner," Jesus will hardly become estranged. The sinful nationalist on the other hand does not regard himself as weak, but as strong, he is *essentially self*-righteous and presumptuous, he despises humility, declares hatred of the enemy to be necessary, has his own conception of honour other than the Christian, is in a word alienated from the figure and spirit of Christ to the point of utter lack of comprehension. Logical nationalists and militarists frankly state in fact that Jesus and His teaching seem to them soft, womanly, unheroic ; they rightly perceive that here lies a world diametrically opposed to their own. They are so estranged from the *spirit* of Christianity that they can hardly be called Christian any longer.

A further pastoral consideration reinforces the necessity to devote more attention to the fifth commandment than hitherto. In combating evil, one should not fix one's gaze predominantly on the particular evil in question, but on the opposite good. Let us preach less about sins and more about virtues ! When we have laid bare how foreign and hostile to the spirit of Jesus is the martial and nationalist spirit, we can show how near and akin thereto is the positive reverse side of the picture. In the section on the religious character of the Peace Movement it was pointed out with reference to the teaching of St. Thomas, that peace, while not a " virtue " in the strict sense of the word, but rather a state, is yet an act and a fruit of love, and so in a certain measure the confirmation of love and its completion. Its presupposition is Sanctifying Grace : a proof of the *dignity* of the peace-ready and peace-making disposition, of its close union with Christ, the author of grace, and with the Holy Ghost, its dispenser and content.

May we not conclude from this that the absence of peace as possession and as act is an ominous sign for man, and its presence a good sign ? There exist *degrees* in the state of grace and in piety, degrees in the imitation of Christ and in being Christian. We speak for example of a " Eucharistic line," and understand thereby the narrow border inside the Church which separates frequent receivers of the Holy Eucharist from the infrequent. Both are equally " Christians." But in their relationship with Christ there is a not inconsiderable difference. Only one who has crossed the " Eucharistic line " and dwells perpetually in the circle of discipleship enclosed by it, belongs to Jesus as a privileged friend. Might we not speak in the same way of a " pacifist line " ? [1] Is it not a residue of " world," " blood," " race," when these natural elements, be they only of an emotional character, hinder or render more difficult the getting over of national differences and tensions, when his worldly, racial, egoistic blood drives a person as it once drove Peter, to seize his sword, in order to fight for the right by *this* means ? Is there not lacking here the sign of a wholly purified Christ-like disposition ? We believe in fine that such a " pacifist line " does in fact exist, and that no one is a complete Christian until he has crossed it (repudiate though he may the word " pacifist "), until, that is to say, he thinks and feels about the use of violence, and about nation, fatherland, " enemy aliens," exactly like Christ. " Feeling " here is more important than " thinking."

Though this may imply a high conception of ethical and Christian conduct, that does not necessarily mean that it can only be looked for at the *end* of a Christian development. Here too the spirit bloweth where it listeth. The ascent of the inner life is not effected rung by rung, like the climbing of a ladder. One attains to love through righteousness, another to righteousness through love, with one the way leads from purity to Christ, with another from

[1] In spite of its unpopularity and ugly associations we can hardly dispense with the word " pacifist," since, as distinguished from the weak and colourless word " peaceable " it expresses an avowed opposition to the notions " militarist " and " nationalist."

Christ to purity. It would be quite wrong psychologically and pedagogically always to begin by
preaching the imperfect in order to rise by strict
logical steps to the perfect. If the preaching of the
Gospel does not achieve the results we desire, the
reason is very largely because far too little attempt
is made to bring home to the people the higher
conceptions of this Divine revelation, and we content
ourselves with stressing only the primitive duties,
often in their rudest form. There was no need for
Christ to come in order to attract " decent people,"
" good citizens," " respectable women," " gallant
soldiers." All that existed and exists outside
Christianity, without Baptism, without Confirmation,
without Holy Eucharist, without priestly ordination.
The Catholic preacher and pastor should have
higher aims. If he pursues them, if he refuses to be
content with having the spiritual resting-place of his
flock remain on a good bourgeois level, if he makes
them familiar with the reaches of Christianity that
range high above and beyond it, he will find that
sermons, for instance, about the virginity that is
bound up with Christ, engender more purity and a
nobler moral sense than the loudest thunderings
against immorality ; that descriptions of voluntary
poverty ensure more respect for the seventh commandment and more contentment than the severest
threats against thieves and misers ; and he will find
further that by dwelling on the glory of Christ as
King and Shepherd over all men and nations, by

preaching love and humility in national relations also, by demonstrating that here no less than in private life violence breeds violence, whereas the spirit, faith and love can even triumph over seemingly insoluble complications—by taking this line, he will find that in the cure of souls too the saying holds : " Good is stronger than Evil " (St. Thomas Aquinas). The noble, the high-minded, yes the heroic has a stronger appeal than the average, the commonplace, and the more or less obvious. That one has the right to meet violence with violence and in self-defence even to use weapons, that an injured person and an injured people are justified in demanding strict satisfaction, a tooth for a tooth—all that a policeman can make clear better than a priest. If the people are to believe that there is something more in a priest than a spiritual policeman, then his discourse must move on a higher level.

Those who have least understanding for the new language of peace—it is the age-old language of the prophets and of Christ—are usually the people whose decisive impressions were formed in militarist pre-war days, and on whom not even the experience of the war has imprinted deeper impressions. Nevertheless, thousands of those who took part in the war have since become pacifists, even though only very few have organized themselves as such, and they have been joined by many persons of a younger generation. Surprising and gratifying is the new peace-spirit that exists among a large section of the *youth*. True, another large section has become thoroughly imbued with the old militarist and nationalist spirit, but the fact that in youthful circles today there is a wider movement towards the ideal of peace than ever before, is the truly new and epoch-making feature of our time. In youthful vigour, in love for their native land, in the spirit of enthusiasm and self-sacrifice, these young people are not only in no way inferior to their comrades in the corresponding militarist clubs and organizations, but surpass them ; if only because militarism and nationalism always engenders a morbid and convulsive temper, since it cannot conceive of love of one's own people without sharp antagonism to another, and this narrows and poisons the mind and heart. *Gratia supponit naturam.* Here in the anti-war youth is a nature which offers the most receptive soil for the supernatural and supernational thought-world and grace-world of Christ. Here the sower of the seed has before him a field which promises fruit a hundred fold. Nothing of what is naturally attractive to youth needs to be sacrificed, least of all the quite indispensable *heroic ideal*. " We must show that we too have our battlefields, upon which we know, if need be, how to die," lies written on the tombstone of the great Ozana, the devoted worker in the field of St. Vincent de Paul. *Ernst Thrasolt*, the poet and leader of Youth, made this the motto of a circular memorandum on " Manli-

79

ness and Heroism in the New Youth." [1]   The
principles set forth by him deserve to be widely
known in pastoral circles for purposes of discussion
with young people :

> " Heroism or heroic deed postulates a per-
> formance great in itself, although perhaps a
> small thing externally (heroism of everyday life,
> in family, vocation, etc.), a performance that
> attests sacrifice, danger, risk, courage, the
> staking of health, position, social honour and
> public reputation. For true heroism, however,
> this more material element of the performance
> is not sufficient ; there needs to be added the
> formal element as well, the determining view-
> point and motive, the intention and content as
> bearing on the fulfilment of the moral world-
> order . . . to true heroism belong perhaps the
> following positive conditions :
>
> > (*a*) The heroic act must conform to the laws
> > of God and morality,
> >
> > (*b*) must be a service done to humanity and
> > the nation, must be really calculated to
> > benefit both,
> >
> > (*c*) must for the most part at least be selfless,
> >
> > (*d*) must be voluntary.
>
> *Negatively* expressed :
>
> > (*a*) The action must not infringe the moral
> > law (cf. Machiavellism, which justi-

[1] See *Politik und Völkerfriede*, Bericht über den 8. Bundestag des
Jungborn, Vertrieb A. Burgmaier, Amorbach, Unterfranken.

fies and sanctifies an evil means if
employed on behalf of the State),

(b) the action must not be injurious, must not
harm the whole of humanity and the
nation more than it benefits them (cf.
the heroism of a robber-chieftain, Hero-
stratism, Berserkerism),

(c) the action must not be performed mainly
for the sake of the reward ; the heroism
is the greater and purer morally, the
less honour and glory there is to be got
out of it,

(d) the heroic action must not be performed
under compulsion. Enforced heroism
is not heroism, it demoralizes. Coercion
to heroism (e.g., compulsory war-service)
is contrary to nature and unethical."

On the basis of these principles, Thrasolt comes to
the following conclusions :

" As Pacifism affirms nation and fatherland
and moral hierarchy of values, as it rejects
modern war precisely because it is not defence
and does not observe the hierarchy of values,
Pacifism alone still offers room for true heroism.
It needs heroism, yes it needs all the courage of
which old Ernst Moritz Arndt speaks, all the
civil courage which Bismarck denies to the
Germans, to set oneself in absolute opposition
to the enthusiasm for war, to the calculations

and gambits of the war-game, to the armed preparations for war, to the propaganda of lies and hatred and the inflaming of popular passion, to current slogans and prejudices and to the whole trend of public opinion—to oppose these things in face of social ostracism, of being labelled unpatriotic, of having the reproach of cowardice and effeminacy flung at one, to resist war to the point of refusing to fight and of refusing to follow all leadership and directions that lead to war, all this requires heroism of the highest order. So much heroism does it require that only very few absolute pacifists exist. Besides this heroism, which is so necessary today that without it a world-catastrophe is inevitable, Pacifism exhibits the heroism of the Cross, of everyday life in family and calling, and of devoted self-giving in all contemporary needs, exhibits the heroism of the spirit, of love, of the struggle for truth, right, social justice and a new order of society, exhibits the heroism of explorers, discoverers and researchers (cf. Nansen, Piccard, Röntgen, etc.), and the heroism in the service of all the blessings and values, which are laboriously built up in the course of a thousand years and then destroyed in a single day by the " heroism " of militarism. Pacifism alone points to the hidden, blessed fields and battle-fields of the earth, those of the Cross and of the spirit of love that issues from the Cross, the fields of honour which seem to be eternally stigmatized with the folly and scandal of the Cross, yet on which alone the redemption of mankind from the evil of war as of all other evils will ripen."

The only thing that strikes one as strange in these pronouncements of Thrasolt's is, that he should also include the last-mentioned forms of heroism under the conception of " Pacifism," and even of " Pacifism alone," whereas in point of fact they are no less open to a militarist. It is quite true, however, that Pacifism, if its principles are consistently carried out, offers a peculiarly good soil for Christian heroism. To illustrate this truth by word and deed is one of the most important tasks of the Christian Peace Movement and of the Clergy.

Let us begin by educating the *children* for peace. That is the easiest line of approach and the one which offers the best prospects of success. Not that children are particularly disposed to peace " from the cradle " as it were ; on the contrary, they are quarrelsome, obstinate, selfish and sometimes display a shocking barbarity towards deformed and defenceless people old and young, even towards the poor and towards defenceless animals : one notices the manifestations of Original Sin more in children than in adults, who have been disciplined by education and a hostile environment. But everything is still flexible in early childhood, and the early influencing of this flexible material is therefore as

G 2

remunerative as it is necessary. It is our duty to avoid anything that serves further to stimulate the aggressive instincts in children such as we have just described. As we know, people pooh-pooh the campaign against war-games and war-toys, but this gives proof of an astonishing lack of psychological knowledge. Even without the lessons taught by modern experimental psychology, it might seem pretty clear that the world of thought and feeling of young children is hardly likely to be less influenced by the constant playing of war-*games*, conducted as often as not with heat and temper, than is the world of thought and feeling of grown-ups by a real war. When boys play at " war," when they group themselves into friends and enemies and call the enemies " French," " Russians," " Poles," whom they must " shoot dead," this means nothing at all for external reality, but for the spiritual reality it means an awakening of political friend-and-foe conceptions, and a making light of deeds of violence and death which is fatal for the forming of moral ideas. Only the ignorant will treat this as a laughing matter and remark perhaps : Oh, the boys don't mean anything by it. Of course they don't. But neither in the majority of cases do grown-ups " mean anything by it," when as politicians and journalists or merely as members of the general public, they charge their heads, hearts, pens and tongues with hostile passions, and in this way prepare war at any rate psychologically—until before they know where they are they are faced with the stark fact that it is there ! Oh, they didn't mean that ! God knows, they didn't want that ! It is precisely this thoughtlessness and naïve complacency that must be made to disappear, and we must begin with the children. The educator should explain to the child exactly what it means to kill a person who has a father and mother or is himself a father, as happens in war and as is jokingly assumed in games of war. He will also permanently enrich the child's soul, if he says to it : " The French are not our enemies ; they are just as good people as we Germans ; there are quite as many bad men who want to injure others among us as among the French."

In such methods of education, however, it is not necessary to deprive the child of every form of contest, of every game in which the fighting spirit enters. That would be to stifle a natural instinct that is good in itself and to stunt valuable physical and spiritual forces. But just as there is a great difference between contest and war, so is there also between games of contest and war-games. In playing at war the child's soul already gets accustomed to regard a person as an enemy simply because he belongs to another country. And the war-like form of contest already exists even in childish war-play, inasmuch as the violence of the stronger carries the day regardless of right or wrong, and without any ideas other than those of external might and armed strength emerging in the child's soul. Instead of which, value should be set on a really *chivalrous* form of contest. This consists in respect for one's opponent, in consideration for his person, especially if he is the weaker, and for his cause, especially if it is a just one. The chivalrous settlement of a conflict is the opposite of the war-like, since the latter consists in making the enemy harmless at any price. To awaken joy and pride over successes gained in this manner is to poison young souls. There is no patriotic interest that could justify such a scandal. If historical instruction, which is imparted almost entirely from a nationalist party standpoint (and is therefore unscientific) is used to pervert the moral judgment of the young, then religious instruction must make good the damage. Today there are many possibilities of fostering the spirit of truth, of justice and of peace. The Peace Movement has thrown bridges everywhere across national and political antagonisms and prepared ways for children to reach the hearts of the children of other lands. (This matter is dealt with more fully in the penultimate chapter of this book.) The spiritual director who calls the attention of children to these ways and means, and tries to help them by arranging, for instance, for them to start a correspondence with children of other lands, will experience a great joy, enrich his religious instruction, and resemble the Good Shepherd, Who " out of the mouths of infants and sucklings has perfected the praise " (Matt. xxi. 16) which adults denied Him, not least because of His opposition to certain "national" views.

(c) CHRISTUS CAPUT

Christ as King stands above us. Christ as Shepherd stands beside us. Christ as Head stands within us.

From each of these aspects of Christ issues a movement that creates peace and demands peace. Especially is this so with the movement that proceeds from Christ as Head of a body whose members are, or ought to be, all mankind. The dogmatic foundations are clear. Christ not only lived on earth for thirty years, but continues His presence in another form to the end of time : morally through the continued reign of His spirit in the government of the Church, as also of the " Logos spermatikos " outside the Church, eucharistically through the Holy Sacrament of the Altar, mystically through the communication of grace to souls that open their doors to it. In this communication is poured forth nothing less than the actual supernatural life of Christ, not in such manner as though the life communicated subsisted in separation from the communicating source, but the two flow together as a supernatural organic unity, like the sap of the vine-stem and the branches, like the blood in the head and limbs of a single body.

We have only to comprehend these mystical

unities to realize how they form a compulsory frame and cement for a peaceful living together of Christ with His members and of the members with one another. The sole possible conclusion to be drawn from such a complete communion of being is the one drawn by St. Paul, the theologian of this profound truth : " Walk worthy of the vocation in which you are called, with all humility and mildness, with patience, supporting one another in charity. Careful to keep the unity of the Spirit (an intellectual unity) in the bond of peace (a unity of will and act). One body and one spirit : as you are called in one hope of your calling " (Eph. iv. 1–4). In an organization of such rich and varied structure there are, of course, naturally-conditioned polarities and tensions between the individual members and groups of members composing it, but no *hostile* oppositions among these individuals, sexes, classes, nations and races. " There is neither Jew, nor Greek : there is neither bond, nor free : there is neither male, nor female. For you are all one in Christ Jesus " (Gal. iii. 28). He for whom this deepest essence of the Christian community exists only as a pale abstraction, who conceives the Christ-Church merely as a big house with many storeys and divisions, where each can go his own way without bothering about the others, and where two people can hate, despise, strive against and destroy each other, such a one " has not understood his faith. He has stuck fast in an individualistic religion, he has not yet advanced to the conception of religion as the act of a community, which is precisely what constitutes the essential nature of Catholicism." [1]

Unfortunately, however, vast numbers of believers have not grasped the nature of the Christ-community even as a theory, much less brought it to bear on the practical ordering of their lives. The whole argument of Father Stratmann's book, *The Church and War* (1924), was built up on this idea. World-peace was deduced from the dogmatic fact that the universal Church as *Corpus Christi mysticum*, as unity of faith and love, as possessing unique authority, must first in her ecclesiastical kingdom, and so among Catholics of all nations, preach and promote peace as a strict command with all the means of instruction and pastoral pronouncement and discipline at her disposal ; that this Catholic Peace has, or rather would have, every prospect of becoming the nucleus of world-peace ; that, on the other hand, inside this supernatural community—though it may include any number of national communities of nations and States within it—a hostile policy aiming at the injury and destruction of another, represented, sanctioned, and put into operation by Christians, is plainly contrary to nature and gravely sinful ; that inside Christendom, in the words of Clement of Rome (ad Cor. c. 47) war is a " rending of Christ's members, a rising up against our own flesh," and therefore " madness " ; that in such an event Christ

[1] Raoul Plus, S.J., *Christus in unseren Brüdern*, Regensburg, p. 11.

Himself becomes the seat of war, so that the obligation to oppose war to the uttermost follows as a matter of course for all Christendom. The possibility of a just war was not denied. But it was pointed out that under present conditions the presuppositions and requirements laid down by the Catholic moral theology, if a war is to be just, can never in practice be realized, and moreover that the party who contrives a technically just war is guilty of the same crime as a man who deliberately contrives an unjust execution. In every instance therefore we are faced in practice with military actions to which both parties contribute, so that in every case moral guilt is incurred by both parties. Hence not only the Catholic moral law but the natural law itself, though most powerfully the principles of Christianity, compel us with the utmost stringency to oppose every concrete instance of war.

In this place we are merely concerned with the consequences that follow from the doctrine of the *Corpus Christi mysticum*. The opposition aroused by the above conclusions recapitulated here from *The Church and War*, goes to show how little the doctrine underlying them lives, and is felt as something that ought to be lived, in the consciousness of otherwise believing Catholics and even of theologians. In an article *Regi pacifico : Thoughts on Education for Peace in religious instruction*, which appeared in the *Katechetischen Blättern* (December, 1929), the editor, Professor Dr. Josef Göttler, writes : " Father

Stratmann lays special weight on the idea of the *Corpus Christi mysticum*. He handles it with great insight and thoroughness. But I do not think we can hope to make the impression he anticipates from it, particularly among the young. Moreover, his exposition is not free from exaggerations. It is not true to say that in the world-war we made war on our fellow-believers, on our brothers. Catholics did not confront each other as Catholics, nor Christians as Christians, but as members of different States. Such exaggerations are apt to effect the exact opposite of the results desired. Properly speaking his argument applies only to wars between wholly Christian, or ultimately perhaps purely Catholic States, and in the strictest sense, only to the medieval struggles between Pope and Emperor and about Papal territory, and to the feuds between ecclesiastical princes and their subjects. Such an argumentation must inevitably lead to a Confiteor and to an apologia not always easy, and sometimes indeed impossible, to maintain. Only in a positive application (as ideal aim of humanity) can I attribute any real significance to this truth."

A discussion of these objections should help to clarify the position. If the sublime mystery of *Corpus Christi mysticum* makes little " impression," this merely shows what a pale existence it leads in the hearts of the faithful. The only conclusion to be drawn from this for the clergy is the obvious necessity of giving more room in catechetics and sermons to the most elementary Catholic dogmas, even at the expense of moral homilies which, owing to their good bourgeois character, can also be given in any non-Catholic community. It is a sad state of affairs when such a fundamental dogma as that of the Mystical Body of Christ, which unites in itself a fullness of religious ideas—in that it expresses the most profound notions regarding the nature of the Church, the nature of the continuity of Christ, the nature of grace, the nature of the Christian community-life—is hardly known among Catholics. Shallowness and ingratitude lie in that forgetfulness. No wonder our Christianity is so externalized if the Christ-community is no longer lived beyond the always only transitory mode of the eucharistic communion.

And how does it stand with its being an " exaggeration " and " not true " to say that " in the world-war we made war on our fellow-believers, on our brothers ? " The question is, whether Catholics and Christians " who confront each other as members of different States," can ever strip off their supernatural being as joint-members of the Mystical Body of Christ, or even so much as leave it out of consideration. When do they confront each other *as such* ? Either always or never ! They are not members of Christ only when they pray or communicate, but also in every other situation of their lives. When two blood brothers fight with each other, they do not do so " as brothers," but as

92

enemies, rivals, business competitors, nevertheless it is fraternal hate and fraternal enmity that we must charge them with. The doctrine of all Christians belonging to one another as members of one body, was first carried over into secular life by St. Paul. When a Christian indulges in unlawful sexual intercourse, he does not do so as a Christian, but as carnal man, and yet he thereby " makes the members of Christ the members of a harlot " ! " Know you not that your bodies (not merely souls therefore or just spiritual abstractions) are the members of Christ ? Shall I then take the members of Christ, and make them the members of an harlot ? God forbid. Or know you not that he who is joined to a harlot is made one body ? " (1 Cor. vi. 15–17). This extreme application of a dogma to life, which, had it not the authority of St. Paul, would most certainly be felt as objectionable and vastly exaggerated, affords the most striking proof that the assertion that in the Great War Christians slaughtered one another not only as adherents of a State, but also as members of Christ is no " exaggeration," but Pauline logic and as such of dogmatic force.

For the rest, early Catholic times hardly reckoned with wars of Christians against Christians. Of this, certain liturgical prayers provide fairly conclusive evidence. Read carefully the votive Masses " Tempore belli " and " Pro pace." In the first you will find that the praying community afflicted by war regards itself as *God's people* resisting the " gentes " ;

in the Introit the " God of Israel " is invoked against
" inimici nostri," and in the Gradual is said :
" Liberasti in brachio tuo populum tuum, filios
Israel et Joseph." God's people, the new Israel,
is today the Church of Christ in her totality. It
seems to us therefore not to comport with this
spiritual unity, when priests of the *same* people of
God, Germans and French let us say, in a Mass
which is intended for *all* " Israel," pray not in a
common intention for protection against a *common*
enemy, but with contrary thoughts and aims
directed as it were against one another ; when they
drag national enmities before the altar of the same
God, declare their cause for " just " as against that
of their brothers, and imagine that they are acting
" by the direct order of Christ "—as it is put in an
explanation of this Mass—when they pray for the
victory of their own side and so for the overthrow
of the other.[1] Similarly the Missa " Pro pace "
lets it be quite clearly understood what kind of wars
the Liturgy has in view, when it grants belligerents
the aid of its intercession ; the Secreta runs : " Deus,
qui *credentes in te populos* nullis sinis concuti terroribus :
dignare preces et hostias dicatae tibi plebis suscipere,
ut pax a tua pietate concessa *christianorum fines* ab
omni hosti faciat esse securos." Thus the praying
Church has in mind wars of non-Christians, Turks,
for example, against us Christians.

[1] Cf. the chapter, " Waffensegen," in the book of war-memories
entitled *St. Michael* (Deutsches St. Michaels-Verlag, Würzburg, 1920).

And so we come back to the fact which Professor Göttler mentions : that there have been " wars between wholly Christian and purely Catholic States " as, for example, those between Popes and Emperors, and between ecclesiastical princes and their subjects, and that such wars must on Father Stratmann's theories " lead to a Confiteor and to an apologia not always easy, and sometimes in fact impossible, to maintain." Professor Göttler has understood aright Father Stratmann and those of us who agree with him. With regard to such wars we hold a Confiteor to be in fact extremely suitable, and a defence of them to be equally unsuitable and impossible. There exists only *one* true defence of the Catholic Church : that of her glorious *idea* and that of such Catholic reality as accords with this idea, which, thank God, may be truly said of a great part of this reality. An apologetic which should aim at glossing over the non-accordance of Catholic idea and reality would have nothing to justify it either from an ecclesiastical or a pedagogic point of view, and would fully deserve Harnack's title of a " lying apologetic." Even in schools the points of contradiction between the Catholic idea and Catholic reality should be duly characterized, lest the knowledge that later years bring of the many short-comings of the Catholic past and present, result in the wheat's being rooted out with the cockle.

Explanatory considerations like the foregoing

prove once again how full of tensions and difficulties is the relationship in which Christianity and nationality, Church and State stand to each other. Much has already been said on this matter in the sections " Christus Rex " and " Christus Pastor " ; here it calls for further treatment from the viewpoint that Christ as *Head* has not only imposed on all nations the duty of respecting the frontiers between State and Church, of keeping the commandment of love, and so of acting in a certain way in each particular case, but has also united them in a permanent unity of the closest kind in His spiritual love.

Among the wholly new, not previously existing, specifically Christian developments that marked the advent of the Church of Christ, was the cessation of every national and State religion in her domain. The new religion was the bond that united all peoples in a higher unity. Formerly the exact opposite was the case. " Religion was one of the principal factors serving to keep the nations sharply divided against each other." [1]

Accordingly the breaking through of Jewish and of every other national-religious particularism was one of the first and most essential deeds that the Church accomplished. No nationality suffered any violation of its rights and distinctive character, but something higher was set above it : the cupola of the universal Church. The order of precedence

[1] Ignaz v. Döllinger, *Geschichte und Kirche*, Albert Lanpen, München.

expressed in this picture, the recognition that the nation lies *under* the universal kingdom of God, must live in every consciousness that lays claim to the name Christian and professes allegiance to the Church. The nation as such need not fear any sort of encroachments therefrom. Its own existence and peculiar type are also from God, who has made men and peoples different. Each nation is a special thought of God, an expression of His wisdom, to each He has given a special disposition and destination for the journey.[1] The fostering of separate nationality, the concentration on a limited space, the material and spiritual exploitation of the national soil, serves not only for the development of the individual, but also for the enrichment of the whole. The plenitude of forces which God has planted in the spirit of peoples will be better worked out through a steady penetration into the deeps than through a dispersion of energies far and wide on the surface. Precisely today, when technical culture makes communication with all and sundry, even the most distant, so easy, the fixing of one's mind on the near and immediate is doubly called for. In cases, too, where a nation exists in dispersion, as in numerous minority districts, it is no contradiction of the higher conception of unity, if, when all just and reasonable measures have been taken to fit them into the political structure of the

[1] For this, and what follows, see the sections " Patriotism " and " Love of Mankind " in *The Church and War*.

State of which they temporarily form part, the cultural possessions and legal claims of these minorities are protected with particular care. This again is to the true interest of the larger Power set over them. The smaller group which is allowed to maintain and foster its personality helps the larger one in which it is imbedded to a deeper understanding of right and humanity, besides giving it the opportunity of completing itself through contact with another type.

The question, however, is, where *today*, in a period of forced and extravagant nationalism, lies the *most urgent* task, especially for the Clergy. No one can complain today of the neglect of the national, the natural and even the primitive. In Germany especially the primitive and instinctive has been emphasized and practised through National-Socialism in a manner that can hardly be surpassed. The priest who would be with Paul " all things to all men," likes to take a middle line and favours the principle of " doing the one and not leaving the other undone." Nevertheless the division and confusion of spirits demands from the priest too a clear decision and an emphasis on one rather than the other. In a discussion I had with some priests on the religious mission of Peace, a colleague with strong national leanings maintained that the first question I must ask myself should run : " How do you stand to the national community of the German people ? " To which the only answer could be : " Just as I stand to my family ; but here I can see no question ; the family and national connection together with the natural feelings of attachment that go with it, is something we all accept as a matter of course." The " question " only begins when this almost instinctive attachment comes into contact with other, perhaps higher interests. It seems to me that " the first question should run," particularly with a priest : Where do I take my stand if the national community of the German people comes into conflict with these interests ? With the interests, for example, of a neighbouring national community, or with those of the Church ? Should one's own people even then be the final measure of one's standpoint ? Most decidedly no ! The only unobjectionable standpoint then is that of the justice which is set above all nations equally. Is it certain that one's own people are in the right ? The neighbour people maintain that *they* are ! There must be something not quite in order, when on the basis of a strange belief in their own press and government, practically the whole German clergy are convinced of the justice of the German case, and the whole French clergy of that of the French. It borders on the comic. There is no question of the bona fides on either side. But of the bona ratio.

Such one-sidedness comes from the fact that we do not stand *above* national things, but *in* them or rather—as there is nothing objectionable in that—

H 2

below them ! In the political sphere too, which is not by any means identical with the national. Quite often there are elements in politics repugnant and inimical to the nation, which profess to act in the name of the people and turn the still, tender affection we all feel for our native land into a blatant hate-filled nationalism. But because the boundary between nationality and State, between cultural and politico-economic interests is often hard to define and to maintain, the person who has his roots in the national life easily finds himself involved in political passions which make him blind. In the chapter " Priester-und Volkstums-Bewegung " of his richly significant book *Das deutsche Volkstum und die Kirche*, Georg Schreiber speaks of the prominent rôle that falls to the priest in virtue of his pastoral office and of his rootedness in the national existence and in popular movements. He goes on to say : " Exaggerated nationalisms have it is true reproached the Church with displaying a blighting indifference in regard to national concerns, when the nation finds itself in the midst of special dangers and developments." [1] It seems to us that such reproaches, which are easily answered, need not be taken nearly so seriously as the counter-accusation that priests participate *too much* in the representation of national interests. Professor Schreiber hints as much himself when he writes further on : " It will sometimes be difficult enough for these (priestly) supporters of the

[1] *Op. cit.*, p. 83.

national feeling to keep the right measure. There have been unfortunate *oversteppings* of the field of activity appointed by the Church, which had their roots in national chauvinism." We could indeed adduce many examples thereof.

Again, every Catholic house of God should strictly preserve its character as a place of worship of the supra-national universal Church. The indigenous national culture and native habits and customs can and should find place in this framework, but not anything that might offend members of another nation, or so much as cause them to feel that they have no home in this house of God. It is even questionable whether national banners of victory are in place in Catholic churches, partly because it contradicts the spirit of unity and love when over the same event there is mourning in one church and rejoicing in another, but principally because it is always very doubtful whether the victory of one State over another is pleasing in the eyes of God. The Church dishonours herself when, without more ado, she adopts as her own the views of the State with which she happens to be living in the same area. National politics, especially during and after a war, are in numberless cases criminal politics. Against such politics, but also against "that unqualified worship of success," Bishop Ketteler has written some trenchant words : "We can only deeply deplore it when we see religion implicated in, and sharing the responsibility for, such policies of State as in their character and ends are divorced from God and God's law. This does not strengthen religion, it weakens it. It is also a deplorable tendency of the last three centuries to expect religion and the ministers of religion to give a religious consecration, so to speak, to all the deeds of violence of politics. For how many victories have Te Deums been sung, from the unjust wars of Louis XIV to those of Napoleon, which were not in praise of God, but which, on the contrary, God in heaven abhorred ! How must God in His eternal truth and righteousness abhor the attempt to make Him in some sort the accessory of human deeds, which are directly opposed to His eternal law, to His eternal command, to His Divine Will ! The higher religion stands, the better it can serve the world, and the more use it can be to the different States as well. Even in its own interest the State should not require this attitude from religion. These official prayers, these Church feasts of jubilation and thanksgiving, do no good." [1]

Bishop Ketteler may serve as an example to every bishop and priest of how he ought to keep his distance from his State and his nation. The strongest interest and the warmest participation in their destinies demands precisely that he should not identify himself with the ruling currents of the moment, not even though they be directed by the government and carry with them the socially most

---

[1] Wilh. Em. v. Ketteler, *Deutschland nach* 1866, in der Auswahl von Mumbauer, Kösel und Pustet, 1924.

respected classes of the community. Especially in foreign politics one's own State is always a party, so that the chance of its being 100 per cent. right is improbable to start with. Whosoever lays claim to intelligence and fair-mindedness must take up a standpoint that lies *above* parties : the standpoint of pure Right. One speaks of a right that one has " as a German," " as a Frenchman," " as a Pole," and is at pains to establish that right as against the right of the other. The only course to which no reproach attaches and which is alone consonant with the dignity of a man who would be blameless, is to seek not the *German* right or any other national right, but *the* Right, and to rejoice over a triumph of the national interest only if that triumph is at the same time a victory of justice. In the other event, one ought rather to grieve thereat, what though the whole nation were singing Te Deums in celebration of victory. The Catholic priest has here a quite special responsibility, he has simply and solely to ask himself what Christ, as common Head of the warring nations, thinks and wills and feels, and to keep his own thinking, willing and feeling entirely free from national and political party interests. God's right over-rides State-right ; there is no State-right against God. A true patriot is one who labours zealously for this God-conformity of his people, who loves them as God loves them and hates them as God hates them, who serves them as God wills that he should, and refuses his service when

God demands such refusal. In such a manner loved and hated and served and laboured the Prophets, who were the greatest of all patriots, but also the most misunderstood and persecuted by their own people.[1]

Anyone who professes a universal *Weltanschauung* like Christianity, must always keep before him the fact that States and nations are only parts of a vast whole and can therefore claim only a relative right. Relative in a double respect : in relation to the other parts of this whole and in relation to the infinitely superior rights of the Kingdom of God. As regards the living together of nations in contiguous or mixed territories, everyone must realize today what a great part the *artificial* sharpening of antagonisms often plays where *natural* points

---

[1] Cf. *The Church and War*, p. 245 ff. In his profound treatise, *Nation und Kirche*, Alfons Adams says with admirable point : " The pantheistic thinker will never be able to establish an opposition between the life of the nation and that of the person, because the same divine substance is operative in all ; the individual will never understand the surrender of life for the sake of the whole. Christian thought, however, demands the affirmation and the denial of the life of the nation at the same time : affirmation when the community lives from the truth, and the life of the community is a walking in the presence of God, but denial when the community serves the idols of the time. This denial of life in the service of a higher truth is at bottom the deep affirmation of the nation, since it takes place not in pride of superiority and contempt, but in solicitude for the true stability of the nation. He who sets up hostility between himself and the ' national spirit ' is no dead or rebellious member of the community. The living member of a community is he who sees the errors and aberrations in a people and freely admits them against the opinion of the many, not he who in a false, blind infatuation sees only good in his nation. He, however, who only denies and does not show the world whence salvation and true life comes, is not worthy to be called a member of his people." *Das Siegel*, Jahrbuck katholisches Lebens, 1926, Kösel und Pustet.

of dispute hardly exist. Fundamentally neither the nations as collective wholes nor their adherents as individuals confront each other as enemies. What Emil Flusser says in his (from a religious standpoint very questionable) book, *Krieg als Krankheit*, is essentially true of all nationally-mixed territories, and especially therefore of frontier districts : " I live on the language-frontier of two nations whose ceaseless conflicts fill the columns of several daily newspapers local and foreign. The people, however, Germans and Czechs, bear no ill-will to one another and do not quarrel with one another. Only the party newspapers do that. In the clash of economic competition the cry is sometimes raised that the Germans should support German concerns, and the Czechs, Czech. That has nothing to do with national enmity, it is one of the unpleasant means employed in the struggle for bread. Nor do the two peoples by any means avoid each other, but everyone does his best to understand his neighbour who speaks a different language from himself. Never is nationality the cause of personal rows and friction. That was confirmed to me by a leading magistrate who has gone into this question very thoroughly. Practically never do disputes come before the court which have their origin in national antagonisms. The people themselves know no language question. Everyone talks as best he can and as it pleases him, and no one objects save only the government offices. These

make difficulties in order that the huge machinery
which is supposed to serve the language question and
the language regulations may find work and justify its
grant, and so as to prevent the many people for
whom this machinery provides jobs from having
nothing to do and becoming superfluous." [1]

In such districts the priest has a task which
though heavy with responsibility is not without its
rewards. He must keep before his eyes the incontestable truth that much of the discord is purely
fictitious, emphasize and foster the natural community of interests, represent with calm determination the pure justice that stands above parties, and
soften this justice with charity. In practice, this
is tantamount to declaring his absolute *disinterested-
ness* in all national disputes. It would be a veritable
redemption if, for example, all priests on the
German-Polish frontier declared that they regarded
themselves not as pioneers of German or Polish
culture, but of Christianity alone, and declined every
participation in purely national strivings, including
membership in the organizations connected therewith.

An educated man can arrive at such an attitude
without the religious impulse. The education of
the mind and heart teaches him the narrowness and
questionableness of the national principle, particularly when it is misused to stimulate acts of political
and economic aggression and sets in motion the

[1] E. Flusser, *Krieg als Krankheit*, Verlag Paul Riechert, Heide i.
Holstein, 1932, mit einen Geleitwort v. Albert Einstein, p. 30.

passions of hate. When this happens we have, even with the highest civilization, a deep-seated inner *unculture*, such as Goethe speaks of in a well-known passage of the *Conversations with Eckermann*, which everyone in this age of nationalism and autarchy would do well to take to heart : " Altogether national hatred is something peculiar. You will always find it strongest and most violent where there is the lowest degree of culture. But there is a degree where it vanishes altogether, and where a person stands to a certain extent *above* nations, and feels the weal or woe of a neighbouring people as if it had happened to his own. . . . The love of country which we are supposed to have derived from the Ancients is with most people a caricature. Our life leads us not to isolation and separation from other nations, but to the greatest possible intercourse with them. The whole trend of our culture, of the Christian religion itself, leads us to union, co-operation, submissiveness, and to the practice of all those social virtues which involve self-sacrifice and self-denial, even to the point of renouncing the feelings, sentiments, nay rights, which we might possess under more primitive natural conditions."

The natural nobility of this standpoint receives supernatural purification through immersion in the wonderful truth of the Corpus Christi mysticism. The nations, too, as member-*groups* can and should belong to it. If they do, then they deserve our love and reverence ; if they do not, they still deserve our compassionate and helping love, but not that blind partiality which sees nothing but merits in one's own nation and extols it above all others in distressing displays of self-laudation. With every nation existing in isolation—a wrong and unnatural state of affairs which was unknown in the Christian Middle Ages—it is the priest's function in the name of the First Commandment to see that the value of the national principle is reduced to its proper level. If there is anything that belongs to the *Vanitas vanitatum*, it is inflated national pride. But what prevents so many of us from giving resolute expression to this view is the notorious sense of inferiority that possesses Catholics in relation to the rest of their fellow-countrymen, who with good reason see in nation and State their highest blessings. Where Catholics are in the minority, as in Germany, England and the United States, there frequently prevails a positively unworthy, almost pusillanimous fear of being regarded as insufficiently " national." The English and Americans tell us that this is the main reason why the Catholics of Anglo-Saxon countries give such feeble support to the strong Peace Movement in those countries. In Germany it is not much better, for here, too, the statements of " national " circles regarding the lack of patriotism among Catholics are still taken seriously and tragically. In France, Italy and Poland there are no Catholic minorities, but to make up for that the Catholic majorities are all the more nationalistic.

When will this spiritual sickness, this religious and Catholic loss of dignity and nerve, cease? Only when God, the Creator and Father of all nations, again occupies the first place in the thought and feeling of these nations, when living religion renders superfluous every substitute for religion (such as nationalism) ; when Christ is again acknowledged as Head of a spiritual body which towers above every other community in worth and dignity ; when the separatist spirit once again yields place to the Holy Spirit of unity and peace in the Christian family of nations.

Whether this end is attained or not, the obligation for the individual Christian to serve it remains the same. Truth subsists independently of its following. Often indeed men do not follow it because it is not proclaimed loudly enough and with sufficient devotion. Here the Clergy can prepare the way, if they are first filled with the right spirit and hold themselves free from false nationalism. Of course many laymen serve this error far more extravagantly, but when the priest serves it, he does so *more deeply,* because he bases everything on spiritual principles, and because his authority gives everything he does the appearance of right. Not from every priest can one expect the transcendant attitude of an Augustine, of whom a historian says : " Everything national is a matter of indifference to him. He makes short work of the Roman Empire. All that remains is the majesty of the victorious Christian faith ; it is the great inter-

national of the Kingdom of God that occupies him."[1]
It is perhaps an overstatement to say that everything national was a matter of indifference to him.
No doubt it was so under the aspect of the national
but not under that of the religious. And to this
extent every priest can and should imitate the great
Bishop. No domain of creation and of life can be
separated from the religious, not even the national.
The whole point is to contemplate *all* nations from
the religious standpoint, the good in them and
the bad, but preferably the good. In this way
we shall overcome the national pride which
blinds a people equally to its own faults and to the
virtues of its neighbours. Even towards nations we
can practise *humility*.[2]

Humility is a disposition of the will to bow before
God and before everything that is God-like in one's
neighbour. All goodness is God-like. Whereas the
proud man has a preference for the less good, is
eager to blame and grudging of praise, the humble
man rejoices at every excellence in another and sees
in it a gift of God. Exaggerated national pride can
only bring itself with great difficulty to recognize the
good sides of another nation ungrudgingly and
without envy. Only a loyal and humble character
that is eagerly accessible to all goodness can do this.

[1] Theodor Birt, *Charakterbilder Spätroms und die des Modernen Europas*,
p. 380, Leipzig, 1920.
[2] Cf. Hyacinth Woroniecki, O.P., *Reflexions sur l'humilité et son
rôle dans les relations internationales* in *Bulletin Catholique International*,
I., 9.

In the tense, poisoned atmosphere that nationalism has created, the priest should make a point of dwelling on the good and great qualities of foreign nations, as they are embodied perhaps in some of their illustrious men. Happily in national presumptions and tensions ignorance is more to blame than bad will. Thus proper enlightenment will not fail of its effect. Love and humility are the binding and harmonizing forces in human society. Were they first fostered in the Catholic religious community above and beyond all political and national frontiers, then from this beginning the whole world would speedily ripen to a more wholesome international life. But hitherto this Catholic example has been lacking.

IV

THE CHURCH AND THE PEACE MOVEMENT

IV

THE CHURCH AND THE PEACE MOVEMENT

(a) THE CHURCH'S COMPETENCE FOR THE WORK OF PEACE

IF the Church were nothing but the still living Christ, the keeper and unfolder of His thoughts and commands and the dispenser of His grace, then there would be no need to supplement our expository remarks on " Christ and the Peace Movement " with a further chapter on " The Church and the Peace Movement." But by " Church " we understand not only this Divine stream of thoughts and grace which flows out of Christ through the centuries, but also the *human* element that mingles with the Divine. From this mingling is formed the visible concrete Church. The human side in her is through the close union with the Divine raised above the purely-human, but not otherwise than in the grace-filled human being. Both, in spite of redemption and sanctification, are subject to the tragedy of the " twofold law " : one striving upwards to Christ, " the Head," and the other " in the members " striving against this higher law. For the Church consists in all her visible members of the children of God

12

and Adam, yes the children of God are the children of Adam in one person, they are all, from the Pope to the last layman, in one and the same person citizens of two worlds : the Kingdom of God and the kingdom of the world. Accordingly everyone separately, and as a result thereof the Church in her totality, bears in himself the tension that irrevocably exists between these two kingdoms. This tension should and can be kept in proper equilibrium. But that is still more difficult for the Church as a collective whole than for the individual members. In the domain with which we are here concerned this is demonstrated specially clearly. The Church as bride, as mystical body of the Prince of Peace is "our peace" (Eph. ii. 14). Her head can only "think thoughts of peace" (Jer. xxix. 11), her heart can only pray for peace, as the Liturgy unceasingly does, but, as we have said, the world-wide body of the visible Church not only *embraces* the States and citizens of this world, but *consists* of them. There is no Catholic who is not at the same time a German, or a Frenchman, or an Englishman or an Italian, or member of some other nation, and there is no Catholic Church in any of these many States, which has not at the same time grown together with that State. This interlacement brings about a community not indeed of spirit but of destiny. In the conflicts of States one with another the German Catholic thinks and feels not only Catholic but also German, the French, French—it is something if they do not put their nation first and their Church only second—and because the leadership of the Church in the Papacy and Episcopate has to reckon with this dualism, nay is itself drawn into it, it is uncommonly difficult in the questions and problems of international peace to maintain the attitude which the spirit of Christ and Catholic thought in its purity demands. The temptation, sometimes perhaps the compulsion even, to compromise in face of the national demands is always extremely near.

Nevertheless the Church can and must be firm in this matter. She *must* be, because the care for peace belongs to her most elementary duties. There is not a war but is ushered in, accompanied and followed by a flood of sins ; every war stands in crying contrast to the " Peace of Christ in the reign of Christ," and is therefore anathema to the Church and must be combated by her to the uttermost. Obviously it is not enough for this to happen when war is already there ; it is necessary to work for peace and against war *beforehand*, to concert active measures to *prevent* war.

This too the Church can do. She is the greatest and best Peace power in the world, if only because she is the most comprehensive and unitary organization. There is not another that is in any way comparable to her. The purely national unions are of course ruled out from the start. But none of the international unions either disposes of such favourable prerequisites for the bringing about of a true international Peace. If for example we compare with the Church of Rome the two other world-organizations that strive for this end : the *League of Nations of Geneva* and the *Communist International of Moscow*, the complete superiority of Rome is at once apparent. Both the other institutions embrace, at least for the time being, only a relatively thin stratum of society : the Geneva organization is at best restricted to an upper governmental and intellectual class, while that of Moscow, though certainly resting on a far wider basis, is in principle an organization of the proletariat. Besides, the form of administration, propaganda and ideology that proceeds from these central bodies is far too uniform ; it takes too little account of the very different views and requirements of the various countries, and is thereby prevented from taking a deeper hold of the peoples. The Catholic Church on the other hand combines an unrivalled *centralism* with a widely extended *federalism :* the separate members and member-groups (dioceses, parishes, orders, ecclesiastical provinces) lead an individual life of their own like the organs of the human body, and yet are bound in strictest subordination to the central head. This means—apart from any supernatural consideration—an unexampled natural comprehensiveness, unity and possibility of unitary influence and activity. The ultimate direction of this universal Church rests in a single hand, that of the Pope. No other person on earth disposes of a similar authority. In his Encyclical *Ubi Arcano* (1922) Pius XI deals with the difficulty of establishing and ensuring world peace through any of the existing worldly authorities : " There is no institution among men which can impose on all peoples any code of common laws, adapted to the present time, such as was possible in the Middle Ages by that true society of nations which was the community of Christian peoples. . . . But there is a Divine institution able to safeguard the sanctity of the law of nations, an institution both belonging to and at the same time superior to all nations, endowed with supreme authority and venerable for the perfection of its magisterium : the Church of Christ, the one institution capable of undertaking so heavy a charge."

Added to this is the fact that the Catholic Church is not only the greatest *natural organization* in the world held together by authority and obedience, but also a *supernatural organization* which by the power of grace is capable of overcoming the human insufficiency that remains in spite of everything. Much that is not possible even to the Catholic Church as a natural world-organization, is possible to her as a supernatural world-organism, as *Corpus Christi mysticum*.

Thus there can be no doubt that *potentially* at any rate this Church is the most important Peace power in the world. That she may become so *actually* two things are necessary. Peace must be *commanded* by the ecclesiastical authorities. It can be done by instruction, exhortation and decree, directly through Papal pronouncement and indirectly through injunctions to the bishops. It only requires a stroke of the pen for a pastoral letter denouncing war and advocating peace to appear in every diocese, or for the chief pastors of frontier districts, where tension is greatest, to come together for mutual discussion regarding ways and means of removing prejudices, misunderstandings, dissensions and the danger of war that lies behind them. But the most effective method is *prohibition* and *excommunication*. What can be done in this way is shown by the Pope's procedure against the *Action française*. The most influential laymen and priests supported this nationalistic false teaching and organization ; the Pope forbade it under pain of excommunication, and the poison tree withered to its roots.

It is often said that the Church is powerless against war ; that it is for the States to prevent it and to put an end to it. Here I may quote a remark made to a well-known clerical professor of my acquaintance by Mr. Newton D. Baker, American Minister of War in Wilson's Cabinet : " If the Churches forbid war, the Governments cannot carry it on." Thus here we find the opposite opinion expressed : it is the ethical not the political power which must decide the issue. In fact there will be an end of the moral élan which has hitherto animated most soldiers, if the ethical and religious powers deny it nourishment, if they stigmatize war as " murder " and " suicide," as has already been done by the last two Popes. Of course only clear vetoes would have decisive effect. By virtue of her " potestas directa " the Church cannot pronounce these, as the policies of States (including their war-policies) do not directly belong to the domain of the spiritual authority ; but underlying her " potestas indirecta " is everything that concerns the moral life. Accordingly in the first thousand years of the Church's existence the Councils and Bishops some-times imposed the severest penalties for participation in war, even in a " just " war.[1] Later they estab-lished the principle—so severely threatened again today—of the inviolability of non-combatants. The carrying of arms was forbidden to the vast multitude of tertiaries of the Franciscan order, a measure of such far-reaching political effect that through it " a blow was struck at the heart of Feudalism . . . and thereby the whole hostile power of the godless emperor Frederick II was weakened." [2]

" Of great importance too were the frequent interventions of the Holy See under Innocent III at the beginning of the thirteenth century, who claimed for himself a right of intervention not *jure feudi* but in virtue of his duty as supreme guardian

[1] Cf. Stratmann : *The Church and War*, p. 141 ff.
[2] Hilarin Felder : *Die Ideale des hl. Franziskus*, p. 291, Paderborn, 1924.

of moral principles, as the Father of Christendom who has to proclaim peace." [1]

In the following centuries Rome as a rule restricted herself in international conflicts to such mediating activities as were desired or at least accepted by the States themselves. The great collection of documents, *Das Friedenswerk der Kirche in den letzten drei Jahrhunderten*, which appeared in 1927 under the editorship of Josef Müller [2] reminds us in the Preface, of the sixty volumes of " Peace nunciatures " emanating from the seventeenth century, and draws attention to the fact that the Holy See " has been the first permanent supreme court of mediation for the nations, of which world-history has knowledge." The efficacy of this authority was greatly diminished as a result of the religious rupture of the sixteenth century, which tore away whole States from the paternal authority of the Pope and smoothed the way for State-absolutism. Strangely enough it was Bismarck who, through his appeal to Leo XIII in the Carolina dispute, inaugurated a new period of Papal mediations in the cause of peace. This reached its highest point with the activities of Benedict XV in the World War. The peace labours of this Pope did not stop at practical intervention in the course of the war itself, but greatly contributed besides to the theoretical elucidation of the new

[1] Karl Doka : *Kirche und Völkergemeinschaft*, p. 19, Haas und Grabherr Augsburg, 1930.
[2] *Deutsche Verlagsgesellschaft für Politik und Geschichte.*

problems of international life that now presented themselves. Thus Benedict strongly supported the idea of a League of Nations, reminded the world that the evangelical precept of love also applied to the relations of peoples and States, and generally throughout the whole of his pontificate emphasized nothing so much as the duty of Peace. His successor, the present Pope, is so alive to the exceeding urgency of this duty for our time that he has made the " Pax Christi in regno Christi " the motto of his Pontificate, and never ceased to demand that the dangers threatening world-peace be removed.

(b) THE APOLOGETIC AND PASTORAL INTEREST IN THE CHURCH'S WORK FOR PEACE

The Church is a mighty reservoir of forces for peace. If however the powers here latent are to pass wholly into act, it is not enough for them to be released by the teaching and pastoral office, *their adoption and application by the hearing Church* is also necessary. The subordinate organs, priests and laymen, must respond to the instructions and exhortations that issue from above. Here much remains to be done. Well might the anti-clerical Clemenceau exclaim with biting sarcasm to his French compatriots : " It is not the Encyclicals of the Popes that we cast into the teeth of the Catholics, but the fact that Catholics do not obey these

Encyclicals ! " Indeed the Catholics of all countries have not as yet associated themselves with the ideas contained therein, or utilized the various other spiritual and organizational energies standing at their disposal for the work of world-peace, with half the zeal we have a right to expect. In an appreciation of the late Protestant Archbishop Soederblom,[1] Max Pribilla, S.J., expresses the opinion that "in the organization of peace Protestants indisputably take precedence of Catholics." And he goes on : " However much we may deplore it, it is nevertheless the plain fact that Catholics are sadly behind in the work for the betterment of international relations, and in proportion to their total numbers exercise a really disgracefully small influence. True the Pope has again and again raised his voice for peace, national reconciliations, disarmament and a fair adjustment of reparations, but the echo was lacking precisely where it was most necessary and might have been most effective. *No leader was found on the Catholic side of sufficient stature and international prestige* to convert by propaganda and organization the Pope's exhortations into practice. Despite the endeavours of a few idealistic individuals and groups, a short-sighted and narrow-minded nationalism obscured for many Catholics the mighty task which, arising out of the terrible needs of the time, confronted them. So it came about that *they missed a*

[1] *Soederblom und die ökumenische Bewegung*, Stimmen der Zeit, February, 1932.

great opportunity for the enlistment of their forces. Instead,
after the war, of putting themselves at the head of
the Peace Movement, and bringing their influence
to bear in that direction, they allowed humanity to
march calmly towards the disaster by which it is
today almost everywhere threatened. The *Osservatore Romano* characterized the actual situation in
discreet but quite unequivocal fashion, when, in
recalling the Peace message of Benedict XV of
August 1st, 1917, it gave Catholics some bitter home
truths to reflect on. In its issue No. 196 of August
24th–25th, 1931, it wrote : ' On the fourteenth
anniversary of the imperishable message we would
ask ourselves a pregnant question, which is at the
same time a serious examination of conscience :
Have Catholics been true to the ideals of Benedict
XV, which are also the ideals of the Church ?
Have they done what is necessary to keep this
message alive, to realize it and cause it to be realized ?
And what has been their attitude towards the international institutions which the great Pope solemnly
approved of, and which originated if not in allegiance to his ideals, at any rate not outside their
range and their light. Granted the defects, which
these institutions had from the beginning, and
granted the necessary reservations that must be
made in regard to them before they can be incor-
porated in the programme of Benedict XV, what
following and support have they found among
Catholics ? Have Catholics allowed their attitude

towards them to be guided by Papal ideas, or have they not sometimes followed the currents of an unbridled nationalism condemned by the Church? The answer to this question or rather to this complex of questions cannot be entirely in the affirmative, indeed on some points and in many respects it must be a complete negative. This question of course is really bound up with that other : Whether Catholics in the international field have taken the place which their principles and the great and momentous demands of the hour require of them.' "

We offer no opinion as to whether Catholics have shown less zeal in the cause of world peace than Protestants ; but that they must devote themselves more zealously to this task in the future than has hitherto been the case, will be denied by no one who realizes how closely the mission of Peace hangs together with the whole Mission of the Church. Of the religio-ethical importance of Peace for its own sake we have already spoken at some length. A word must here be said about the *apologetic and pastoral interest*. We teach that every man of good will, even the non-Catholic, can recognize by certain marks, which is the true Church of Christ. Christ himself has declared the qualities of His heritage that prove it to be His. The society founded by Him must be *one* in faith and in love ; *holy* in its doctrine and in its members ; *Catholic*, i.e., universal in its extension over the whole earth, and *apostolic* in its continuity with the doctrine and authority of the first vicars appointed by Him. The examination of the two last marks will soon put the earnest seeker after truth on the track of the Roman Catholic Church. Also the unity in faith and the holiness of doctrine are not difficult to recognize. But the unity in love which was described by Christ as the most essential characteristic of His disciple-ship? "By this shall all men know that you are My disciples, that you have love one for another" (John xiii. 35). If today a non-Christian and non-Catholic seeks for this love among Christians, can he find it? Will it fare with him as with the Pagans and Jews of the first centuries, who were really overcome by the love shown by the Christians of that time, and were moved thereby to enter the Church? "If," remarks Emil Fiedler, "an educated Chinese or Japanese or Hindu travelled through Europe with the Gospel in his hand, in order to take a look at the peoples who have been Christian for the space of fifteen hundred years, it would require a threefold miracle of grace for this foreign visitor to become a Christian. And were he, after reading the Gospel, to read nothing but the history of Europe, he would be forced to the conclusion that Christianity in Europe has failed, and that the White race must be worse than all others, whose history has not been more bloody, whose morals have not been worse, but whose religion has only been Paganism." [1]

[1] *Defensive oder Offensive?* I., p. 101, Rauch, Wiesbaden, 1929.

A mass of weighty evidence can be adduced in support of this view. In his book *Nationalism*, the great Indian poet Rabindranath Tagore, a man of world-wide reputation and influence, puts before the eyes of the Japanese, so intent upon European culture, a picture of that culture which reveals the utter contempt that this heathen feels for the Western culture imported into the East. Of course Tagore would be the last man not to recognize the high values latent in this culture, but what he cannot understand is the fact that the pioneers of European culture rob and exploit peoples of alien race with the most brutal violence without reproof from the representatives of Christianity, nay that the imperialistic and militaristic *Gewaltpolitik* goes hand in hand with the Christian Mission. When they keep down " fallen races which struggle to stand on their feet, with their right hands dispensing religion to weaker peoples, while robbing them with their left—is there anything in this to make us envious ? Are we to bend our knees to the spirit of this nationalism, which is sowing broadcast all over the world seeds of fear, greed, suspicion, unashamed lies of its diplomacy, and unctuous lies of its profession of peace and good will and universal brotherhood of Man ? " [1]

The Chinese priest Yong-An-Yuen, O.S.B., has contributed several articles to the Esperanto journal, *La Juna Batalanto* (1927), in explanation of the

[1] Rabindranath Tagore : *Nationalism*, p. 94 (Macmillan).

hostility of Chinese students to Catholicism. "The deepest reason," he asserts, " is excessive nationalism. Not only antichristian students, but all Chinese, whoever they may be, are agreed in this, that Christianity has been introduced into China through the cannons and machine-guns of foreign imperialistic Powers. We can write articles in Chinese news-papers till our fingers are sore, proving that Chris-tianity is absolutely independent of all imperialistic Powers—the heathens simply do not listen to us." Latterly Alfons Väth, S.J., has drawn attention to the compromising results which the warring of Christian peoples has called forth among the heathens : " They observed the White race butcher-ing one another at their very doors. A feeling went through the coloured world as once among the Redskins : We barbarians are after all the better people. The last remnants of respect for the White race disappeared. Unfortunately respect for the religion of the White race also sank ; for all the White nations call themselves Christian. English missionaries helped in China to recruit coolies for France, where the majority of them perished miserably. This and similar examples aggravated the contempt and hatred." [1]

Pagans exist not only in distant lands. In the middle of the erstwhile Christian West a generation of *Neo-pagans* is growing up which is becoming

---

[1] Alfons Väth, S.J. : *Das Bild der Weltkirche*, p. 131, Hanover, 1932.

increasingly estranged from Christianity and whose adverse criticism is directed solely to its fruits. It is our firm conviction that millions of European unbelievers are *bona fide* when they charge the Christian Churches with not having preserved the spirit of Christ. Many of them reject the Christian teaching of faith and morals as such ; with these we are not here concerned. But there are many others who direct their attacks not against this teaching, for which on the contrary they have a great respect, but against what they are sincerely convinced is the betrayal and falsification that takes place through its theoretical and practical accommodation to the powers of this world by numberless representatives of Christianity. Intellectuals and proletarians are at one in this conviction. In a " Letter to a Catholic lady " (*Weltbühne* of February 4th, 1930), Ignaz Wrobel meets the protests often raised on the side of the Church against the injurious criticism of people of his type. Wrobel makes the following counter-protests : " Do you show any regard for *our* feelings ? I, for example, feel hurt when I see a Catholic priest standing in front of soldiers, gaily and cheerfully inciting to murder, debasing and degrading the gospel of love to the gospel of the State—it offends my ears. Who takes *that* into consideration ? Not *your* people, Madam ! "

A strong light is thrown on the frame of mind that exists in *proletarian* circles by the following document. The Berlin members of the League of

Peace of German Catholics had arranged with the Fellowship of Reconciliation (*Versöhuungsbund*) for a peace message to be sent by German children to French children. The text concluded with the angelic praises of Christmas night. The father of one of the teachers sent the Fellowship of Reconciliation the list of children whom his daughter had gained for the idea and added the following remarks : " I had hoped to win far more children for this good cause, as in the first instance I had promised myself good results from a canvass in my daughter's school. Unfortunately, however, an obstacle presented itself, which I had certainly suspected in a vague sort of way, but had not taken sufficient account of. We live in Wedding among an almost exclusively proletarian population. These people have met with untold disappointments in their lives, have had to witness, if not endure in their own persons, any amount of undeserved misery, a want and distress in face of which the Church and the State have always failed them. The Church for the most part only offers phrases and exhortations, references to a life beyond, while her representatives in the vast majority of cases give loyal support to capitalism which cares nothing for the life beyond. All these matters are of course not new to the Fellowship of Reconciliation, nor above all is the failure of the Churches in regard to war. I merely recall them in order to make you understand why it is that these people, whose whole life is a heaven-crying indictment of all the institutions of a complacent bourgeois society, reject with an *indescribable hate*—let us call it by its true name—not only the Church but everything that has anything to do with religion. The people are against war, are in favour of promoting a good understanding between nations, and similar efforts on the part of Socialist bodies have received considerable support from them, but their mistrust of bourgeois or for that matter religious organizations is insuperable. It is a pity ; for the children themselves would have gladly joined in. At a meeting of parents I argued the matter out with them. I begged them at any rate not to disappoint their children. I am sending you the letters, but urgently request you to see that these letters are addressed to Socialist working-class families. . . . Perhaps it would have been better in the wording of the message of reconciliation to frame the concluding sentence with its strong religious colouring rather differently. After all, the important point is, what we do and the spirit in which we do it, and not that we use the name God which is holy to one, but to another—and not necessarily the worst type either, since he values truth and honesty more than a symbol sanctified by tradition—has no significance whatever, unless indeed it stands for a false deity used by the ruling class to force the weak more easily under their yoke. Precisely we of the Fellowship of Reconciliation ought to be conscious of the great guilt that the Churches of all denominations have incurred in the course of centuries ; and should serve our mission without making a long story about it. Yes, I believe that the ' Church ' is past saving, and that true religious life will perhaps quietly develop again if we clear the soil of rubbish and break it up, if without fine phrases we humbly serve a new humanity, as the brothers and sisters in Lichtenstein or elsewhere have done and still do.''

In this chapter we are concerned not with the rebutting of distorted and unjust, because generalizing charges, or with the justification of our own standpoint to ourselves, but with a sober evaluation of the spirit we meet on all sides and which we have to deal with *pastorally*. The only way in which we can effect anything in this direction is by making conciliatory advances, by quietly explaining the true facts of the situation and by removing all misunderstandings, and also by frankly and humbly admitting the numerous mistakes which have been committed on our side in our perhaps enforced alliance with the political and military powers. We can truthfully declare that much of what we, together with all other mourners, are terrified at today, has only been brought home to us by bitter experience, that it has needed the events themselves, of which we could know nothing beforehand, to make us see clearly. But then, too, we must really draw the right conclusions and make a new beginning.

We theologians are wont in our reflections and

judgments to proceed more from *ideas* than from *things*. We think deductively rather than inductively ; we are, without perhaps being quite aware of it or wishing it, Platonists rather than Peripatetics who gather knowledge from looking around them and from experience. For the domain of pure theology the deductive method is certainly the better, and in so far as we have to do with revelation from above, the only legitimate one. But it is otherwise in judging the vast field of the facts of experience of which historical events and the various happenings of the contemporary world form part. Here it is a dangerous matter to approach things with a complete thought-scheme and preconceived ideas instead of proceeding in the opposite way by examining things in their whole reality, and with all their accretions, connections and operative effects. And nowhere is this more important than in judging war and its occasions. Here we fall only too easily into the danger of viewing and manipulating events in such a way as to make them fit into our familiar categories. These categories themselves cannot easily be warped, the facts however can. As when the schema " justum bellum " is so obligingly satisfied by official acts. A " legitima auctoritas " is there, a " causa justa " is there, and a " recta intentio " is there—compare the acts !—nothing more is needed for a " just " war. So it is one's duty to join the army, and all the evils, physical and moral that are bound up therewith must be taken into the bargain. Granted that it is sometimes very difficult to see through the flagrantly immoral content of this formal framework—for that very reason one should hardly dare to take it upon oneself to quash every doubt as to the morality of such warlike enterprises and to preach the incontestable moral duty of taking part in them ! But that is what one comes to, when one has ideas and principles— in this case, those of a just war—" at one's finger-tips," in constant readiness to apply them everywhere and at all times to things—no matter how complicated or little susceptible to such application they may be. After all that past history and contemporary events have taught us, with the monstrously selfish and one-sided policies that States have ever pursued, the presumption of a " just " war cannot possibly stand.

In his sermon on the occasion of the opening of the Disarmament Conference in February, 1932, Cardinal Faulhaber said : " We live in a period of transition ; and just as in other questions, so, too, in the question of war and peace, *a change of heart* will be effected. . . . Even the teaching of moral *theology in regard to war will speak a new language.* It will remain true to its old principles, but in regard to the question of the permissibility of war, it will take account of the *new facts !* " There is no doubt that this " change of heart " has already taken place in millions ; their opposition to war and to the militarism that leads to it has acquired passionate strength and become a sacred command of their conscience. But is the " new language " about war and its permissibility being used by us theologians? Apart from a few negligible exceptions, it is not ! By the overwhelming majority of priests the old and out-moded language of *pre-war* days is still being used about war, as if there were no " new facts " to consider, and this causes the greatest consternation, nay scandal, to large numbers of informed laymen. It is high time—for there are many signs that we are now standing in a new pre-war period—that theologians devoted the same study to the ethics of peace and war, to which the questions of a new international law belong, that they devote to other matters ; that they sought and acquired full information regarding the dirty backgrounds of wars and their preparation, that they recognized the share of the armament industry in working up " national " feeling, in short, that they participated in the " change of heart " and took account of the " new facts." Of special importance is it that the senseless maxim " If you want peace, prepare for war " be abandoned for good and all. It must, as Cardinal Faulhaber said in the same sermon, " be dismantled like an old battleship."

But a mere *theoretical* change of position is not enough. The work for peace and against war must engage our *practical* efforts as well. This is anything but alien to the duties of the pastoral office. True there are souls who not only do not desire this sort of activity from their pastors, but even resent it ; while alongside of those who raise their voice against dragging the Church into military-political interests, may perhaps be ranged such as object to the *pacifist* attitude of ecclesiastical persons. The question is, however, from what standpoint these two classes of objectors proceed. Quite obviously the voices that clamour for a resolute peace activity on the part of the clergy, argue from the Kingdom of God, the dissentient voices from the kingdom of the world ; the former are moved by a religious interest, the latter by a national. That the *true* national interest is not prejudiced by resolute support of the Peace Movement has already been demonstrated and need not be argued afresh. The clergy therefore need not pay any attention to charges of this sort. Especially when his pastoral work lies among the proletariat, the priest will find that his pacifist principles provide the surest road to people's hearts. In a discussion on the address " World Church and World Peace " given by Chancellor Dr. Seipel at the Innsbruck Academic Festival, a well-known clerical publicist criticized the many efforts made outside the Church for improving the state of society, since the universal Church of salvation could do all this so much better : " Associations were formed with wonderful social ideals. . . . I could not help smiling a little and thinking to myself : If only you good folk would bring the people back to the Church ! If only you would guide them to a practical religious life ! " He overlooked the fact that many people, particularly those in need of social help, are so alienated from the Church that they are utterly inaccessible to guidance towards a practising religious life. The question should in fact run : *How* can I bring these masses back to the Church ? Answer : By restoring their confidence in this Church ; and that is only possible if I prove to them that the Church is their ally and leader in questions which for the proletariat are matters of life and death. The proletariat feel their existence threatened by the sacrifices which capitalism and militarism impose upon them, and what embitters them more than anything is the idea they have that the Church is in league with these powers. In commenting on Seipel's speech, the Socialist *Innsbrucker Volkszeitung* gave passionate expression to this bitterness : " Certainly in past centuries man has not succeeded in preventing wars, but this was not because the peoples were burning to tear each other to pieces, but because their rulers, supported by the spiritual power of the Roman Church, had the liveliest interest in the kindling of wars. And if fatalism has gained the upper hand among men and the idea of peace is laughed at as Utopian, the chief blame rests with the Church which, as the spiritual power, has always ruled the minds of the masses and still today holds them in large measure under her jurisdiction. . . . If according to the Church to which Dr. Seipel belongs there is no Divine condemnation of war, then the masses of the people, who in and through war have had to endure such inhuman horrors and want to prevent a repetition of these horrors, will have to revise their attitude to the Catholic Church. For a Church whose spokesmen unashamedly declare that war is not forbidden by God, which therefore formally sanctions war as a necessity and scoffs at genuine pacifism, cannot possibly mediate the true religion." We know what answer we can make to such representations. (We may observe in passing that Seipel himself was a warm friend of the League of Peace of German Catholics and was the principal speaker at their Conference at Frankfurt-am-Maine in 1930. Moreover, in the speech which called forth the Socialist attack, the great Catholic statesman suggested a categorical condemnation of war as a possibility *in the future*.) But no answer will regain for the Church the trust of the embittered masses, which does not reassure them as to the Church's position in regard to war and to the powers that induce it. The surest way of allaying suspicion on this point and of relaxing the tension is for the pastor personally to show himself a resolute opponent of war and of the war-mongering spirit. Priests who serve the Peace Movement are treated with respect and welcomed as speakers even in the anticlerical camp. We know from experience that agreement in the fight for peace is a bridge for the settling of religious differences also, and is thus a truly pastoral means of smoothing the way back for those outside the Church. Indeed the Catholic Peace Movement is never an end in itself, never divorced from the Catholic mission as a whole, but always only part and means of her labours in the Kingdom of God and for the salvation of souls.

V

THE POINT AT ISSUE

V

THE POINT AT ISSUE

ONE who is actuated and "moved" by the opinions developed in this book, certainly does not deserve the reproach of being a light-hearted optimist or a woolly pacifist ignorant of the ways of the world. In our introductory remarks we carefully separated our views from the aims and tendencies of the Peace Movement to which such a characterization might perhaps apply. In summing up the contentions of this book, we think we may say that the pacifist principles we have professed and are fighting for are identical with the views and demands of Christianity on the subject. The Christian is no shallow optimist, but neither is he a pessimist who has no faith in any goodness in the world ; he is a sober realist, who, without illusions, but not without ideals and hopes, looks things, both the good and the bad, in the face. He who has an eye for the good forces at work, cannot but recognize that the numerous anti-war organizations that were formed or acquired new strength in Europe and America after the Great War, no less than the views of leading personalities in political life, do, when all is said and done, point to the growth of a changed inner attitude towards the phenomenon of war. A front, such as was completely unknown in the past, has been formed against war and the establishments that render it possible. A moral front of great, and in part passionate, determination. War today, in contrast with former times, is described by millions as a " crime," as " murder and suicide " ; many thousands are prepared to lose life and property rather than serve it further ; even in international law the way has been broken for an outlawry of war.

The easiness, the matter-of-course-ness, so to speak, of the breaking-out of war, has thereby received a serious check.

But does that mean that the catastrophe has been rendered impossible for the near future ? Unfortunately not. For the forces which consciously or unconsciously make for war, especially the material ones, are still tremendously powerful, indeed have become stronger than they ever were. That is descriptive of the position ; far more people than before have turned away from war and the war-mentality, but the opposing side, too, has immensely increased its qualitative strength. The anti-war front and the war-front alike, are filled with the utmost determination : the one to use all means for the sabotage of war, the other to apply unimaginable methods of violence and destruction. And because material forces work more quickly (if less durably) than moral, the war that has been duly prepared by these forces, with potentialities of destruction that have increased out of all knowledge since the last war, has far better prospects of remaining master of the field than the predominantly moral forces opposed to it. A single squadron of aircraft can effect more havoc than millions of peaceful folk, conscientious objectors and fighters for Peace can avert.

Thus everything is deepened qualitatively. The great majority of people can fondly wander off into the camp of the peace front—modern militarism and armament imperialism can afford to ignore this quantitative disposition ; it no longer needs massed armies ; material of high value qualitatively (the human material of a limited war-élite and the mechanical material of the contemporary killing industry) suffices it. It would almost require a miracle for the speedier dynamic of these war-forces not to get the start of the more gradual one of the forces of peace.

But why then have a Peace Movement at all ? Simply because there is no *certainty* that the war which has been prepared will break out. The possibility of averting it remains and grows in proportion as the forces of peace (which also include those of a material kind) increase in strength. Just as it is the duty of a doctor and sick-nurse to apply remedies in order to preserve, to prolong the life of the patient, so must everyone who feels himself co-responsible for the physical, spiritual and moral well-being of his people and of humanity, do everything he can to help to avert the terrible calamity of another war. But there is another reason far more important than this, especially as the success of our preventive efforts is improbable. It is a question of repudiating war *morally*, even though it prove impossible to prevent it. It is a question of saving our *moral* personality, even though our physical may perish. If it comes to the worst and the insane massacre begins, then everyone who is jealous of his reason, honour and conscience, should be able to confess before God and the world : *I* have had no hand in this ; *I* have *not* helped to bring it about either actively or passively, *my* hands are pure of this crime, I gave warning and worked against it ! (As regards helping to bring it about, we know that *every* sin of whatsoever kind flows into the great judgment of God, so that we all of us, in that we are sinners, help to bring about the judgment of war. But there is a direct and an indirect way of bringing it about. Here we are talking of the direct way. Of this at least we will not make ourselves guilty ; and for the rest, we will strive too with holy zeal to avoid every other sin which indirectly serves to bring down upon us the punishment of war.)

Even more important than this witness before ourselves, is the witness that *Christianity and the Church stand there pure*. We confess here, at the end of this book, that our work for peace and against war and its sources, has no stronger motive force than the impulse to help to save Christianity and

Church, the mystical Christ, from *moral* entanglement in the dark powers of war, should it prove
impossible to save them from physical entanglement
therein. As compared with the moral, the physical
is of no importance. If war cannot be extirpated,
then to this scandal, too, are applicable the words of
Our Lord : " It must needs be that scandals come,
but nevertheless woe to that man by whom the
scandal cometh." In the scandal of war share all
who at the decisive moment, be it only in feeling,
set an interest of the kingdom of the world—by
which we here understand State, nation, country,
worldly honour, worldly gain—above an interest
of the Kingdom of God : God's honour, the keeping
of all His commandments to the point of loving and
blessing our enemies, the Peace of Christ in the
reign of Christ ! He shares morally therein who,
with James and John the " Sons of Thunder,"
would call down " fire from heaven " on hostile
men and groups of men, " to consume them."
" You know not of what spirit you are. The son
of man came not to destroy souls, but to save "
(Luke ix. 54–56), runs the answer. Moral responsibility for the outbreak of war is shared by all who
put their faith in the sword and act accordingly,
instead of reflecting that " all that take the sword
shall perish with the sword " (Matt. xxvi. 52), which
is to be interpreted more in a spiritual than in a
material sense.

Thus on the positive side, our main efforts must be

directed to promoting a deeper and wider understanding of the ideas of Christ in regard to the use
of force. True, these ideas are "foreign to the
world," inasmuch as the world remains eternally
alien from the pure spirit of Christianity. What,
for example, can it make of the principle that " the
evangelical commandment of love which is laid on
individuals is equally binding on States and peoples,"
and that " not only domestic but also foreign policy
must be guided by the teaching of Christ," as the
last two Popes have taught in Christ's name?
There is absolutely no prospect, we may think, of
ever winning the " world " for such a policy ! But
have we Christians and above all, we priests, therefore the right to bow down before the superior
might of the other side, to accept its insolent domina-
tion, nay, to become its allies in our views and
sentiments ? Have we the right to assert that the
practical application of these precepts is impossible
" in this age." For what age, then, did Christ and
the Popes utter them ? Manifestly for our time and
our world. But here we have to state a distressing
fact : in contradistinction to the *social* Encyclicals
of the Popes, which have been given the fullest
consideration and treatment in Catholic publica-
tions, the Papal *Peace* Encyclicals have been almost
hushed up ! This is to be explained by the fact
that while the theoretical turning away from
capitalism has made great progress among Catholics,
the same thing cannot be said of even a theoretical

turning away from nationalism and militarism. Here passion and subjective feeling have too big a say. It has to be admitted, however, that even objectively the situation has been enormously complicated by the close partnership and functional interlocking of Church and State ; the State has avenged itself for the attempt to christianize it in this alliance by secularizing its partner, and now extrication from the entanglement is not easy. The more closely these two life-partners—which also form a unity in the flesh in our individual selves —have grown together, the more difficult it is to recognize and achieve the autonomy, independence and sublime ascendency of the Kingship of Christ.[1] Yet this is a matter which concerns Christian responsibility and Christian dignity, the priestly above all. Without the most personal decision in the increasingly sharp division of spirits, we can no longer preserve this responsibility and dignity. The lukewarm will be " vomited " (Apoc. iii. 16) ! The irresolute, the faint-hearted, those who serve two masters, will be owned and rewarded by neither.

The resolve in this crisis to " stand by the Church "

[1] Among those who have complained of this are to be found some of the most eminent and saintly figures of Church history. That not only a practical but also a theoretical secularization and absorption by the State has taken place is attested by Cardinal Faulhaber among others : " Individual moralists unduly influenced by the peaceful co-operation between Church and State may sometimes insert too much of a State-conception of war into their moral teaching." Faulhaber, *Rufende Stimmen in der Wüste der Gegenwart*, p. 457, Freiburg, 1931.

is right, if by "Church" we understand the right thing. In many cases this term is used to designate everything that bears the Catholic name, and even when so used, it stands of course for a notable spiritual society. Nevertheless this great Catholic mass cannot serve as the standard of our moral conduct ; even the Catholic clergy does not necessarily do so. Just as in the ranks of this order are to be found numerous insufficiencies of other kinds, so here too there exists a fair number of nationalists and militarists of the deepest dye. To " stand by the Church " can in our case only mean : to stand by the teaching and pastoral office which rises to its authoritative peak in the Papacy. " Ubi Petrus, ibi Ecclesia " ! Benedict XV in one of his addresses to the Cardinals, lamented the fact that nationalism had found its way into the highest ranks of the clergy. Thus many a person of strong nationalist sentiments would be able to justify his position by an appeal to this or that high Church dignitary, if these represented the " Church." The only *authoritative* Church is the supreme teaching and pastoral office. But this, through its two last holders, Benedict and Pius, demands with quite inescapable plainness the turning away in principle from the autocratic national Power-state, from its presumptuous arrogation of absolute sovereignty, from its false theories of armed defence, from everything in fact that is commonly understood by " Nationalism " and " Militarism," and a return to the Kingship of Christ, which can only be served by the fostering of supra-national justice, amity and love.

If one asks how this is to take place in practice, the answer is that before all else, the struggle against the evils in this sphere must be taken up by theologians and pastors. If the Pope wishes " priests, as ministers of peace, to be assiduous in this work, which is indeed the very compendium of the Christian life, in preaching love towards one's neighbours, even if enemies, and to afford a shining example by waging war everywhere on enmity and hatred " (*Pacem Dei*), then hardly a day passes without providing some opportunity of fulfilling this duty. In a time so charged with political tension as ours, even conversations at gatherings of every description are wont to be carried on with bitter recriminations against political opponents. In such cases a direct reprimand on the part of the priest will usually be a psychological mistake, and he will do more good by unobtrusively diverting the conversation into other channels. But here as everywhere the best instruction is by example. If the priest himself stands on a high watch-tower, then his mere presence will keep at a distance words against the fifth commandment no less than words against the sixth. It goes without saying that the one are just as sinful as the other, although consciences in regard to the fifth commandment, especially in its deeper aspects, frequently live in

anarchy and are therefore subjectively guiltless.
Instruction on the sinfulness of much political
opinion, language and action should therefore be
given in the pulpit. It should not be difficult to
bring home to the faithful that the settlement of
both party and national differences is no less subject
to the commandment of love than is the settlement
of differences between private persons. But is the
preaching of love fostered with the devotion due to
its central position in the Gospel? Is it carried out
in the right form? We must not deliver our sermons
on love in a hard, loveless, hectoring manner. But
a timid, lame recommendation is also not enough.

Immediately following his exhortation to the
priesthood as quoted above, Pope Benedict proceeds : "And in this connection also they should
exhort and pray Catholic journalists and writers in
that ' as elect of God, holy and beloved,' they may
clothe themselves 'in the bowels of mercy and
benignity,' expressing it in their writings, abstaining
not only from false and empty accusations, but also
from all intemperance and bitterness of language."
That this Christian commandment is often disregarded by Catholic writers also, particularly
journalists, is notorious. We will willingly credit
most of them with good faith, with the belief,
namely, that they are fighting for national right
against foreign wrong. But if all the Catholic
journalists in one country are convinced of the
accuracy of their information and of the justness of

their standpoint, and all the Catholic journalists in another country are convinced of the accuracy and justness of theirs, then this very circumstance throws a characteristic light on the objectivity of these outpourings from the press. It is no use objecting that it is unfortunately impossible for a journalist living in his own country to report otherwise. For we have daily proofs that the same events are handled and reported in one way by one paper, and in quite a different way by another. Even in the most serious conflicts, it is possible to present things in a calm, understanding and conciliatory spirit without thereby compromising objective truth and national honour in the slightest degree. On the contrary, truth and honour are better served by such conduct, as in strife between two parties, truth and right are rarely on one side only.

How does this concern the clergy? It is the duty of the clergy to bring home to Catholic journalists the injunctions of the Gospel and of the Popes ; to pull them up if they go off the rails ; to urge them in a friendly way to be true to the highest standards of truthful reporting and fair interpretation, and to give the same prominence to the faults of their own as they do to the faults of the foreign State. This alone is to serve truth, justice and love, and it is the only service which deserves the name " Catholic journalism." Admittedly, just as every virtue has the " faults of its virtue," so too has peacefulness. The fault of the virtue of peacefulness (" per excessum ") is softness and sentimentality, voluntary or involuntary blindness to real injustice, wickedness and obduracy. It would cease to be a virtue to shut our eyes or even half-shut them to such phenomena. Whoever has to judge of controversial matters, needs clear powers of discernment, a keen glance especially for where the " dolus " lies hidden. A difficult art to acquire. He alone possesses it who has and cultivates within him the spirit of Christ and sees all things with His eyes. In cases where Christ would blame, scold and scourge, the Christian may and must do so also, particularly the Christian teacher, preacher, educator and writer.

The above-mentioned practical possibilities of serving the Peace of Christ are more of a general pastoral character ; ultimately it is a question of serving the fifth commandment of God. Direct co-operation in the apostolate of International Peace might proceed as follows.

1. In the first place moral theologians could oppose modern war far more sharply than they have hitherto done. In the previous section on " The apologetic and pastoral interest in the Church's work for Peace," we drew attention to the words of Cardinal Faulhaber that in view of the altered circumstances " even moral theology will speak a new language about war. It will remain true to its old principles, but in regard to the question of the permissibility of war, it will take into account the new facts." Here and there this new language in

face of the new facts is already finding expression. In his essay *Wieder Krieg von Volk zu Volk?* to which we have already referred, Schilling calls war, as it is prepared today, of nation against nation (instead of army against army), a " barbarous method of thinking and acting," and declares that : " It hardly needs stating that the idea of waging a bombing war from the air against innocent folk, against peaceful citizens, and defenceless women and children is a mockery and defiance of the traditional Christian conception of war, which has always been strictly to confine war within the limits imposed by hard necessity. . . . A government which even so much as played with such ideas ought to be branded by the conscience of the world with the mark of Cain," indeed it " would be even worse than the first fratricide, for it is planning a hundred and thousandfold murder." What we need in fact are the words " murder," " mass-murder," " suicide," " monstrous crime " (Pius XI, April 2nd, 1934). Only, these notions must find a place in our text-books of moral theology together with the full logical consequences to be drawn from them. At the end of these deductions must stand the words " unjust " and " immoral " war. Or is perhaps " hundred and thousandfold murder " not " unjust " and " immoral," and so forbidden in the strictest manner possible ? And if that is forbidden, is not any co-operation therein likewise forbidden ? Why this fear of declaring the murder of millions to be forbidden, when no moral theologian will hesitate to condemn as " murder " under pain of mortal sin and excommunication, the destruction of a single living creature that exists in " embryo " —a creature that has not come as yet into the light of the world, can hardly be considered as vital even, and may seriously endanger its mother's life ?

Schilling wants in fact to see the war " of nation against nation " which therefore is waged *contra innocentes* as well, " forbidden." But he goes on to say : " It is no good objecting that the prohibition of air warfare against the peaceful population, and the maintenance of the principle whereby war is waged between army and army, are half-measures, that we must go the whole way and forbid war altogether. We can do this on paper certainly. But so long as the condition already mentioned is not fulfilled and realized at least in part, we must unfortunately pass over these pious wish-fancies of the extreme pacifists and proceed to the order of the day, fixing our eyes upon men and reality." This distinction between war against the armed and war against the unarmed (" peaceful population," in moral theology " innocentes ") is undoubtedly right in theory. But is it not precisely a " paper " distinction and a " pious wish-fancy " ? After all, it is absolutely certain that actual war today is directed consciously and " directa intentione," and so not " per accidens," also against the civil population. Is it therefore unreasonable and the mark of "extreme pacifism" to demand that moral theology should turn its attention not to an abstract war of theoretical possibility and pious wishes (" bellando pacificus," St. Augustine), which today no longer occurs, but to the modern war of reality, and to declare that what is being prepared today is according to all the rules of morality a " bellum injustum " ? For it goes without saying that we are thinking not of a political prohibition of war, but of a moral-theological and ecclesiastical one.

In an article on *Seelsorge und Politik* in another number of the *Linzer Quartalschrift* (1934, 3), Otto Schilling has no hesitation in writing that the Church has " the right . . . to declare at any time that a specific law is contrary to natural right, and is therefore not binding on the conscience of Catholics. Here the Church makes use of her *potestas indirecta in temporalia*, of her power in the political domain." Can the State issue a worse law than to order its subjects to commit " thousand-fold murder " ?

We think therefore with Cardinal Faulhaber that Catholic moral theology must in fact begin to speak a new language, and that what the last two Popes have already pronounced in the way of general sentences of condemnation on modern war should be translated into the systematic terminology of the schools. The simple preacher and pastor can, however, already begin by making his own the words of the reigning Holy Father, " murder," " suicide," " monstrous crime."

2. Unity is strength. Ideas which appear novel, bold and difficult to carry out, are easier to hold on to, to clarify and spread, if they are fostered in community. Accordingly the clergy should also make it their business to establish or encourage Catholic Peace groups. Where specific organizations are not possible or not advisable, a group of workers could be formed inside an existing association, or the whole association be made to interest itself in the Peace Movement by means of occasional lectures, discussions, and best of all, divine services.

3. Of all possible ways of serving Peace, the most important finally is *prayer*. " Unless the Lord build the house, they labour in vain that build it " (Ps. 126). Prayer must accompany all other endeavours for peace, in cases indeed where for some reason or other no other steps can be taken, it has a high value in itself alone. After the great demonstration at Lourdes in September, 1934, in which 60,000 soldiers of the Catholic front from all parts of the world took part, one of the Germans wrote : " While we German soldiers were returning home from Lourdes, we considered what could be done to carry the spirit of Lourdes into the world of German manhood. Here is the upshot of our discussions on the journey home : We soldiers of the German front must not and will not leave the men at Lourdes to pray alone. . . . Not a new organization with

journal and subscriptions, no, only a prayer movement in the framework of the men's apostolate "
(*Germania*, 1935, 51).

And before that, at the Christmas of 1933 when it
was generally expected that in view of the new
menace to peace from the resurgence of power-
politics Pope Pius XI would resort to some sort of
public protest and summon the Church to action,
he found in the end no other counsel to give in the
conclave of his Cardinals than the exhortation to
" pray, pray, pray " ! Precisely because matters
were so serious, he could think of no other counsel.
Since then the world-situation has become still more
serious. The pioneers of Peace feel themselves
almost at the end of their strength and hope. But
one thing remains : the power and mercy of God.
" I have lifted up my eyes to the mountains, from
whence help shall come to me " (Ps. 120).

Besides the silent supplications which each one of
us can at any moment make to heaven, there exist
numerous liturgical prayers for peace. The Ordinary
of the Mass alone contains four.[1] Even without
these express prayers for peace, every Mass, as the
expiatory sacrifice of Christ, is in itself the mightiest
of all peace-prayers. Nevertheless it is important
that priests and with them the faithful should also
pray for peace subjectively at the Holy Sacrifice.

[1] In the Dominican Mass which deviates in several details from
the Roman Rite, the prayer of the priest before the Gospel runs
(instead of the Munda cor meum) : " Dominus sit in corde meo et
in labiis meis ad pronuntiandum Sanctum Evangelium pacis."

In order to bring this home to them in a special way, in 1931 an *International Secretariate for Masses for Peace* was called into being in Paris at the church of Notre Dame des Victoires (not to be confused with the Cathedral of Notre Dame). The first Masses of this kind were celebrated on February 13th, 1931, simultaneously by a German and a Frenchman : Père Desbuquois, S.J., director of the Action Populaire, and Dr. Brauns, German ex-Minister of Labour, who happened to be staying in Paris at the time. Since then the Mass for Peace has been solemnised in this church every month, and in the course of the same year a number of episcopal cities adopted the same practice. Prince Hatzfeld brought the stimulating idea from Paris to Breslau, to Cardinal Bertram, President of the Fulda Episcopal Conference. This Conference at their August session in 1931 expressed the wish that these Masses for Peace should also be said in Germany on every first (i.e., Sacred Heart) Friday of the month, or the following Sunday. The seed fell on good soil. Owing to the zeal of the Right Rev. Christian Schreiber, Bishop of Berlin, these monthly Masses have met with particular support among the Catholics of the Capital. Here they have been solemnised with sermons in a different parish church each time, so as to make the whole Catholic population of the city as familiar as possible with the work.

Typical too was the arrangement in Duisburg-Hamborn. There a six o'clock Mass on a week day was purposely chosen in order to combine the sacrifice of getting up early with the Sacrifice of the Mass. The number of attendants increased each time, and the vast majority went to Holy Communion as well. In order to make the service as complete as possible, the Mass is celebrated as *Missa recitata.* Among the Votive Masses of the Missal the most appropriate seemed to be the " Missa ad tollendum schisma," which, though it has in view a conflict of a different kind, can also be made to apply quite well to the hostile political conflict of the nations within Christendom, and indeed of all peoples that suffer from disunion. The whole Mass prays for nothing but unity and peace. (The " Missa pro pace " assumes that an actual war is in progress, and so is not quite suitable.) The whole text, inclusive of the permanent parts of the Mass, has been printed on a handy eight-page sheet, so that the whole congregation can combine in prayer with the officiating priest in the most beautiful manner.

Naturally every parish is quite free to make whatever arrangements it likes in regard to the monthly Mass for Peace. It is desirable however that every re-arrangement or new institution should be communicated to the Secretariate. (Address : Secretariat international pour la Paix, a.b.s. de Mons. l'Abbé Jourdain, Curé de la Basilique de Notre Dame des Victoires, Paris 2.) This central office enters the names of groups, priests and permanent members into a " Golden Book," which it transmits each year to the Holy Father in Rome.

Of similar character is the *Union Eucharistique dans le Sang Redempteur* (le culte perpetuel des Messes pour la pacification du monde) which goes back to the noble missionary of the Sahara, P. de Foucauld. This work also engages its adherents to offer up Mass for peace and to arrange for this three times or at least once a year, but calls on them besides to remember this object in their ordinary attendance at Mass, which should as far as possible take place daily. In the foreground stands the thought of the Precious Blood of the Redeemer, to which reverence is done by special prayers. This Eucharistic Union was canonically established in 1932 by the Bishop of Fréjus and Toulon ; it has its headquarters in the grotto of Sainte-Baume. Address : Secretariat de l'Union Eucharistique, la Sainte-Baume, Plan-d'Aups, par Saint-Zacharie (Var). In August, 1934, Cardinal Pacelli sent the work his heartiest good wishes and conveyed the Holy Father's blessing.

INTERNATIONAL EUCHARISTIC PEACE SUNDAY

The thought of entrusting the difficult work of peace to the Eucharistic Christ is so obvious, that naturally many Christians hit upon it at the same time, and differ from one another only in the form of this devotion. What is more natural when going

to Holy Communion than to reflect on the fact that
the many partakers of the Blessed Sacrament receive
the same food, the same Flesh and Blood, and therefore too the same spirit which presupposes and
bestows the same dispositions ; that consequently
feelings of enmity among them would be a contradiction ; that just as they all become one with one
and the same Third, Christ, so too they must become
one among themselves in love and peace ; that they
should therefore think of one another and pray for
one another ! Political boundaries do not exist in
this communion of spirit and peace. But because
boundaries in the world of nations, in which these
Christians united with Christ have to live, exist as
hard facts menacing the Christian life, they must be
spiritually overcome or at least rendered harmless.
The Table of the Lord breaks through all boundaries,
and the souls of those who meet together at this
Table must do so likewise. Doubtless therefore
many have already, without special prompting,
offered up Holy Communion for their brothers and
sisters in foreign lands, i.e., shared its fruits with
them in prayer. And that priests too preach this
idea goes without saying. So we need not be surprised that—without perhaps knowing about each
other—another Eucharistic peace organization has
been formed in addition to the one described above,
on the initiation of a priest : the so-called " International Eucharistic Peace Sunday."

The Eucharistic Table-fellowship of Germans and

Frenchmen was a common occurrence in the occupied districts of France during the war. At that time the French country priest, Abbé Demullier, bade both his own parishioners and the German soldiers pray for one another. When later he came to South Germany as a prisoner of war, his zeal for bringing his own and the German people together increased. He started the " Correspondance Catholique franco-allemande," a small monthly magazine to which the Holy Father gave his blessing on May 7th, 1924. An exchange of ideas was to go hand in hand with the reception of the Sacrament of the Altar for one another. On each first Sunday of the month the French were to pray at Holy Communion for the Germans and the Germans for the French. Abbé Demullier succeeded in enlisting the support of the *Amsterdam Eucharistic World-Congress* of 1932 for his work. The Congress expressed the wish :

1. that all the Catholics of France and Germany who go to Holy Communion on the first Sunday of the month may participate in the intention of the " International Eucharistic Sunday " ;
2. that those who cannot communicate on this day may pray for the same intention ;
3. that as many Catholics as possible of other lands may associate themselves with this work.

The desired extension to Catholics of other lands has been achieved inasmuch as a large number of Poles have joined in a similar Eucharistic fellowship with Germans. At the German-Polish Whitsun Conference held in Berlin in 1929, Father Count Rostworowski, S.J., announced that he had gained 2,000 Poles for this pious practice.

We see therefore that during the past decade, peace has been prayed for more widely and more fervently than is generally realized. It is our sincere conviction that if, despite the often extremely tense situation and despite the threatening preparations for war, peace has been preserved during the last few years, it is owing to these prayers. The frequent conferences of statesmen for exorcizing the war-menace will be without avail, so long as not even the name is mentioned among them of Him Who holds all the threads of world-history in His hands ; nay, it is possible that as a punishment for this truly sinful omission, the catastrophe which they would prevent by purely human means, will break out more surely than ever. Without faith, without humility, without the vital consciousness of the absolute dependence of all earthly things on God, all the cleverness of man will be confounded, precisely because it is nothing but the cleverness of man. " I confess to thee, O Father, Lord of heaven and earth, because Thou hast hid these things from the wise and prudent, and hast revealed them to little ones " (Matt. xi. 25)—a saying which establishes for all time the vanity of all self-assured knowing, willing and doing divorced from God, but also the plenitude of light and strength that comes to those who put their trust in God. This saying of Our Lord's is also a challenge to, and a repudiation of, the wisdom and cleverness of those who seek to built up peace without God, and a hope for those who are " little " enough to know that peace on earth is possible if we give glory to God on high and work for peace in the way and with the means that God has revealed.